REQUIEM

REQUIEM

Shizuko Gō

Translated by Geraldine Harcourt

KODANSHA INTERNATIONAL LTD.
Tokyo, New York and San Francisco

Publication of this translation was assisted by a grant from the Japan Foundation.

The original was first published in book form in 1973 by Bungei Shunjū under the title *Rekuiemu*.

First edition, 1985

LCC 84-48698
ISBN 0-87011-716-5
ISBN 4-7700-1216-0 (in Japan)

It was darker with her eyes open. It's always night when I wake up, Setsuko thought. The air was damp and chill on her cheeks, and on her hands and feet. Did her skin awaken when the world faded from sight? If she stretched out her right hand till it brushed the wet surface of the earth, little eyes at her fingertips could pick out each of the beams and struts holding up the wall. The wall was clammy and unexpectedly soft. Scratching it with her nails made the earth crumble away till she thought it would never stop.

And yet when they were digging the shelter her father and brother had complained of exhaustion.

"What'll we put in the air-raid shelter?"

"Bedding, emergency rations and a first-aid kit."

"Don't forget my trains." This was Hajime's voice. "Put them right at the back, in the leather trunk that was Grandfather's, so they won't get broken."

"Don't be silly, there's barely room to squeeze the whole family in here as it is."

Setsuko had just revisited the little schoolboy her brother had been when, red-faced and pouting with the effort of gripping his crayon, he'd written in white on a string of blackened caramel boxes, "The Benkei Flyer. Hajime Ōizumi. First Grade, Class One." But Setsuko herself had remained meanwhile in her present state: lying helpless, her impenetrably tangled hair full of lice. Little Hajime had been so distant and uncaring in the dream that she could only weep.

"Get me some water, will you, Setsuko?" The whiteness of his teeth when he smiled, and of the towel around his neck, stood out in the darkness. The soil from the shelter had been spread evenly over the yard, and they'd planned to grow vegetables there.

"The land around here was reclaimed after the big earthquake of '23. We might be lucky to get a pumpkin out of it." It was their mother at the kitchen window, her head covered in a towel as she did the housework. Spades and hoes, buckets and planks, hammers

1

and nail boxes were scattered about the tiny garden. Hajime was sitting on the porch with his work boots off, revealing the embarrassing girlish whiteness of his feet, which looked odder still because they had long hairs on the backs of the toes.

"What funny feet!"

"What's wrong with them? They've got five toes, haven't they?"

"But they're all hairy."

"Human beings are covered in fine hairs, you know."

"*Fine*? Call *those* fine?"

They laughed over steaming sweet potatoes. On a warm Sunday in late autumn. Never thinking, then, that there'd come a time when they would use the mandatory air-raid shelter.

Her eyes, her nose, her mouth were hot. Her breath was burning. Had her fever risen? If she kept still it wasn't too hard to breathe. But the thirst was unbearable. Setsuko thought of the pain she'd have to endure for the sake of a drink of water. Her flask had been empty a long time, and thirst had made her wake again and again, but each time she'd thought of the effort and decided she'd rather go thirsty. It was a mere two or three yards from the shelter to the spigot in the ruins of the kitchen. But there were five steep steps between the floor of the half-underground shelter and the surface, and if she turned face down she knew she'd be racked by a violent cough. For she had already fought for breath till she'd lost consciousness many times as coughing fits followed hemorrhages.

I'll suck my finger, like a baby. There might be some moisture in my mouth. Which finger shall I try? The little one looks sweetest, but I'd feel too sorry for it. All right, then, the forefinger. When I was younger, didn't they teach us that this one stands for Mother?

Mother.

A smile like a shadow came over Setsuko's face, as with closed eyes she held her finger in her mouth. Father had said there was only room in the shelter for the four of them, empty-handed, but Mother had found a hiding-place for a small bundle: a length of cheap silk the dark purple color of gentians, with tiny crimson and white crosshatches. A whole bolt. Setsuko didn't know how she'd come by it, or when. "I've got something to show you, Setchan." The air of secrecy in her mother's smile made Setsuko glance around quite furtively. "Look, there's a whole bolt. Twenty yards. Just right for you, Setchan, when you finish high school. It'll make a pair of regulation *monpe*, a jacket and a coat. But we might be able to make matching kimonos for you and the bride at Hajime's wedding." Schools had relaxed their uniform rules since families were unable to replace the items that wore out; instead, schoolgirls were being allowed to wear any loose work pants and long-sleeved jacket. Despite these changes, however, much of the prewar way of life—or something close to it— still survived in those days. Their mother could look forward a few years to her daughter graduating from the girls' high school and her son, then at engineering school, getting married when he had his diploma.

The cloth had gone for fuel to burn their mother's dead body.

Tears fell over the smile still etched on Setsuko's cheeks. Then, before they'd faded, a new smile overlaid the first. Mother, I'll be there soon. Father and Hajime are with you, aren't they? The family will be together. Like old times.

The fingertip she had put in her mouth was dirty after touching the wall. She felt grit on her tongue. It wasn't a pleasant sensation, but as she was working the foreign matter out over her lips with her tongue, a surprising amount of saliva spread from its root. Knowing her right hand was dirty didn't stop her sucking that finger, though. She couldn't change hands, for she didn't want to let go of the small notebook she held tightly in her left hand—not even for a second. Setsuko knew she was going to die. She wanted to die hugging the notebook to her breast. She couldn't tell when the time would come, and so she was reluctant to let go even momentarily.

It was dark, there was no mistaking that. Yet Setsuko suspected she wouldn't have known the difference had it been light. It wouldn't have been at all surprising if she'd lost her sight. She had no idea how much time had passed since that evening at the end of August when, under a beautiful sunset, she had drunk water to her heart's content, letting it splash from the tap over her hot cheeks, then filled her bottle and half crawled back to the damp musty bedding in the shelter. She'd woken a number of times and wet her parched throat until the water gave out, but she had seen no light since that intense sunset. It's always night when I wake up, she had thought—but, she added, perhaps the fact is that I can't see.

What good would it have done her, anyway, as she lay quite still in pitch-darkness? Setsuko gently closed her eyes—and there were images, real enough, but which should no longer have been visible in reality. A flower would appear in all its sweet fragrance, and the cold silkiness of its petals would spring to life before she even stretched out her hand. Someone would come into sight, and in an instant she'd have recreated the way that person appeared to her at every point of her sixteen years. Her train-crazy brother's collection chugged past: from the Benkei Flyer he'd made out of caramel boxes to an elaborate tin diesel engine carefully finished with lacquer, hauling a long, long string of cars on an endless track. Hajime stood and watched the passing locomotives with a pair of Rising Sun flags signed by well-wishers draped over his shoulders and crossed on the breast of his black school uniform. The next moment, Hajime himself was speeding away on the rear deck of a car, leaning far out to wave. He laughed a little self-consciously, showing his white teeth. On the night before he was due to leave, Setsuko had seen him go to their mother for medicine for an aching tooth. The sight of him plumped down on the floor (but towering over his mother), his big mouth open childishly and his muffled voice instructing "No, not there, farther back," had struck Setsuko as awfully funny. She'd

4

laughed till she cried, and then, before she knew it, she was weeping in earnest. Did Hajime still have a toothache the next day? Whenever she thought about him leaving for the front, she was sure the tooth must still have hurt as he flashed that bright smile.

"I've moved to the address shown overleaf. I am well. I hope you are too."

Each member of the family had one of the three postcards (more like notices of a change of address) that had come from Hajime. He had gone off easily, giving no sign of any great resolve, and his letters from the front said not a word of what was in his heart. Their mother had looked at the rows of neat, square lettering that barely covered a quarter of the card and sighed, "What a waste of space."

"It's all right for you, Ōizumi. You can do what you want."

"You don't have anyone else's feelings to worry about, yourself."

The two boys' voices had woken Setsuko from a nap.

"It's not so simple in my case. With my brothers going to the two extremes. After the examples they set, I don't know where I'm going."

"You don't look too worried."

"The smile that hides a broken heart! When I was a kid I knew what I was going to do: go to military school. The neighborhood bullies picked on me after my eldest brother, Shōichi, went to jail. 'The spy's little brother,' they called me. I swore I'd become a general to get even. Just you wait, I thought. But then my other big brother, Seiji, starts talking about joining up. We'd all thought he was going to be a pianist, but he wouldn't listen to reason—it had to be the army for him. That wasn't practical, anyway, because of our eldest brother being a communist. He couldn't have got into officers' school, or the naval academy either. So in the end he dropped out of middle school and became a naval pilot cadet. And was killed

5

in action when he'd barely learned to fly solo. Are you listening, Ōizumi?"

"I'm listening."

"It was back at the beginning of the China Incident, when there was all that excitement about sending in the bombers. We'd been cold-shouldered by the whole neighborhood till then, because of Shōichi, but all of a sudden we're the bereaved family of a war hero. I was only thirteen and didn't understand a thing, but I thought it stank. Then Seiji's last letter reached us. His last message, if you can call it that, was some sheets of music he'd written out—a Chopin polonaise, and part of Schumann's *Scenes from Childhood.* I heard my mother crying as she played them, and I thought: he must have done it to shield Shōichi. They call it 'killed in action,' but it was more like suicide. The polonaise was Shōichi's favorite, you see, and Seiji often played it for him. The Schumann was something my mother used to play in the old days, and we children would all gather round and listen in the music room. It was after this happened that I lost sight of what I should do."

"But now you're the one who's talking about signing up."

"True. But that doesn't mean I'm not confused."

"It doesn't make sense."

"Not confused so much as undecided."

"It's the same thing."

"It's because I can't make up my mind that I'm asking you to join up with me. A lever makes it possible to shift things even if you don't have the strength."

"I'm a lever, am I?"

"Something like that."

The alarm had sounded for an air-raid drill and the lamp wore its blackout shade. "Remember, now, we had the *kotatsu* made for your father's use," their mother had reminded on her way out to a neighborhood meeting. The weather wasn't really cold enough yet

6

to need the brazier under the quilt-covered table; their mother had simply been guilty because she wouldn't be there when their father (who felt the cold) arrived home from working late. He still hadn't got back. Setsuko was dozing with her feet under the *kotatsu*. Hajime and his close friend Shūzō Wakui were sprawled talking on the opposite side. When she woke, Setsuko pretended to be still asleep. The six years that separated her from her brother made such a difference these days that he might have belonged to another species. She couldn't openly share her brother's and his friend's thoughts. She was careful to breathe evenly, while beneath their lids her eyes were agog with curiosity.

"What threw me was this: I asked myself if going to officers' school precisely because Shōichi was branded a traitor wasn't the same suicidal behavior as Seiji's. After claiming for so long that I would go to officers' school, I suddenly found myself choosing engineering. Another big surprise for my parents—here was the son least likely to succeed, and now the only one they had left, choosing a draft-exempt course and offering to take on the family business. So Father and Mother were pleased, in a way. They hadn't wanted me to join up just to be killed like Seiji. They didn't know the real reason I changed my mind."

"In that case, wouldn't it be better not to volunteer now? If you finish school first, so you're ready to take over your father's firm in the future, you'll be doing something worthwhile in its own way, won't you?"

"The future? Think there *is* a future?"

"How can you say that?"

"When I gave up the idea of officers' school, it was because I didn't want to become a soldier merely to die a suicidal death—even if it did make me a 'war hero.' But now I'm not so sure."

"What do you mean?"

"Ōizumi, have you thought about what the redeployment at

Guadalcanal means? Or the Glorious Sacrifice on Attu Island?"

There was no answer.

"Know what I think? I think the Japanese Army is losing. If I'm right, then we'll die anyway—so the sooner the better. If we're going to be forced to die, I've begun to think I'd prefer to go while I can still believe I'm dying for my country."

"What are you getting at?"

"This summer I went to see Shōichi. We'd never talked much before, with him being a lot older, and cleverer too. But once I got to thinking about seeing him and hearing what he had to say, I just had to go."

"I heard he was ill. How was he?"

"Well, it doesn't look like he'll get better. It's a matter now of how many years he has to live."

"He was released, wasn't he, after he changed his views?"

"Listen, there's more than one way of changing your views. My brother 'recanted' only for show. I found that out when I went to talk to him. He's never departed from what he believes. He decided to 'go over' when he began to hemorrhage in prison, knowing that because he was sick he wouldn't be made to collaborate in the war. That was all it meant. His friends who recanted were nearly all sent to fight overseas."

"So your brother won't cooperate, even now?"

"You wouldn't say 'even now' if you could hear him talk! He says it's all turning out just as he knew it would. And he'll never let them send him to his death. Even if the whole of Japan becomes a battlefield, he says he'll keep out of their clutches and stay alive right to the last. He's obstinate as hell."

"Does he think Japan will turn into a battlefield?"

"Within a year or two, he says. We'll lose the ground we've gained, one territory after another, and then be bombed to a cinder. Everyone's going to die, he says."

"So you plan to volunteer and die fighting, if you have to go anyway?"

"That's right. My brother's convalescing at a temple at the foot of Mt. Akagi in Gunma. I thought everything over while I was looking at the gravestones and tablets there. You know, the graves of soldiers killed at the start of the China Incident are terribly grand affairs. You gaze up at a great slab of stone and there, engraved in big letters, it says 'Here Lies Army Private First Class So-and-so.' And the tablets are of glittering gold. Then they get plainer and plainer, till these days you're fobbed off with just a wooden marker. They died for their country too, you know, but look at the treatment they're getting. Now what's the point of dying honorably in battle if there's nobody left on the home front to enshrine you as a god?"

"Cut it out, you idiot!"

"Are you angry?"

"Of course I am. I'd like to knock your block off."

Setsuko's eyes popped open in disbelief—and yet she was half afraid he meant it. She quietly raised herself to see Hajime good-naturedly knuckling his friend's forehead. Shūzō Wakui smiled too as he ducked. But if the room hadn't been so dark she might have seen that Shūzō's eyes, far from smiling, were reddened and moist.

"But what about you, Ōizumi?"

"I'm going. I'm a simple fellow, I know. To lay down my life for my country and His Majesty the Emperor: that says it all."

"You're a lucky man. I envy you."

Though Hajime had decided he was a simple fellow, Setsuko remained sure that his bright smile hid the pain of an aching tooth.

Their father carried one of Hajime's three postcards in his jacket pocket wherever he went, and it had gone missing with him on the morning of the great air raid on Yokohama, when both must have

9

turned to ashes in the flames of the incendiary bombs. Mother's postcard had been placed in her coffin. Setsuko's should still be between the pages of the notebook in her left hand. Though the first two had come addressed to Mr. Yutaka Ōizumi and Family, the last had been, unexpectedly, for Setsuko.

Miss Setsuko (I hope you're grateful),
    Seems my turn has come, so take care of everything. You're a bit cheeky, but capable. I can leave things to you.
                Yours,
                Hajime

Could these be his last words? Couldn't he have written something more? By the time Setsuko held this card in her hand both her father and her mother were dead. The newspapers were reporting kamikaze raids almost daily, so she could easily imagine the circumstances in which he had written. And on every rereading the same bitterness would fill her heart. She took the card out of the notebook, being very careful not to drop it. There was another card which she also took out. Hajime's was creased and roughened, but the other was flat and not as worn. Setsuko knew her brother's card by heart, and she could picture every dot of the neat brushstrokes on the second card, too. It was from the chief priest of the secluded mountain temple where Shōichi Wakui had been convalescing after he'd recanted and obtained his release from prison.

Dear Miss Ōizumi,
    I hope you are in good health and exerting every effort during these troubled times.
    It is my sad duty to inform you that Mr. Shōichi Wakui passed away on July 16 at 4:16 A.M. As he promised at the last that he would take the items you had entrusted to him and give them to

10

Professor Niwa, I placed the two notebooks beneath his pillow in the coffin and cremated the body thus.

Let us join in prayer.

Hot tears coursed suddenly over Setsuko's cheeks—tears of anger. She thought she understood Wakui's anger now. For he'd been right: the war had ended.

When everyone was resolved to die, when everyone had seen meaning in giving their lives for their country and Emperor, Shōichi Wakui alone had called such a sacrifice meaningless. "The war will end. We must wait, hold on till then, protect our lives." She felt the crushing weight of chagrin that must have borne down on him when he realized he wasn't going to make it. The war was still on when Wakui died. But now it was over. The darkness spread and deepened in Setsuko's heart.

How *could* the war simply end?

"Oh, it's quite possible—men started it, after all."

"Even if justice has not been won?"

"Justice for whom, that's the question. And people will still have to go on living after the war's over, you know." Shōichi Wakui was practically the only person Setsuko knew who thought about "after the war's over."

For some time Setsuko kept the fingers of her right hand pressed over the two cards on her chest. Hajime never met Shōichi, his friend's brother. Though his name had come up in that conversation around the *kotatsu*, she'd never had a chance to ask Hajime what he himself thought of the errant older brother. Unable to tell anyone how deeply her own encounter with Shōichi Wakui had affected her, Setsuko bore the painfully intense impression alone. The two postcards were always pressed together; yet perhaps they perpetually ignored each other.

11

Replacing the cards in the notebook, she laid it on her chest again. The gray notebook.

Dear Setsuko,

I've found a nice notebook. Mama turned it up for me in Papa's study. Please note the color of the cover. It's gray. Le cahier gris. Daniel and Jacques. Isn't it wonderful? Mama knew just what the color meant, and she gave me a very significant look and said "Naomi, my sweet, next Sunday you'll get the meals, won't you?" I take after Mama in hating housework, but on Sunday I shall work without a word of protest.

School is duller than ever since your class left. The playground has been dug up from one end to the other and planted with vegetables, and there's no room even to skip. We did the digging, of course. The teacher told us to bring shovels to school. Mama was angry. She said it was stupid. You wouldn't have thought I'd ever take a shovel, would you? But lately I've become very well behaved, due to the influence (need I say?) of Setsuko the model student. When I shouldered my shovel and marched off to school, the teachers probably got an even bigger surprise than Mama.

What a sad mistake I've made. Whyever did I decide to meet you only on every other Sunday? Up till now I've been able to see you every day at school and on a lot of Sundays as well, but Mama was afraid I'd be making a nuisance of myself if I went to see you every Sunday. How do you like that? It's all very well for her to talk. Fancy my mother knowing what the word "nuisance" means!

But I realize that I would be a nuisance now that you're working at a factory and needing plenty of rest on your day off. That's why I'm being quiet and patient. (Though after carrying on like this I could hardly be described as quiet or patient!)

Only the first- and second-year students are left at school. And the second-years are about to go too. It won't be long before we first-years are called up for factory work. We're all being split up. When you were mobilized and sent to the factory, Mama said "Oh, what a waste! Imagine making a bright girl like Setsuko mind a conveyor belt!" But when I told her my turn would come sooner or later, she said she pitied the poor person who had to put me to work. According to Mama, if they knew what was good for them they'd use a monkey instead. What an insult! Whose fault does she think it is, anyway, that her daughter turned out this way?

But I think I've changed a great deal since we became friends. I no longer quarrel with all comers. In fact I smile at everyone. Some people still look at me as if the sight disgusted them, but I don't get angry any more. I tell myself that Setsuko would be upset if I was quarrelsome, and so I put up with the slights and forget them as quickly as I can.

I often think about my fight with Yoshiko Akiyama, how I hurt her, and how you took me to the Akiyamas' to apologize. Afterward you cheered me up even more than it might have done if her mother had forgiven me, when you told me we'd done everything possible to show we were sincere and so shouldn't go on blaming ourselves. How lucky for me that I got into that row while you were on duty. It was beastly of Yoshiko to call Papa a spy, but since it was my fight with her that led to our friendship I almost want to thank her for it now.

I wish I could be like you. You're neat and humble, but when something has to be said you can hold your head up and say it loud and clear, even in front of the headmaster or Mrs. Akiyama. I'm not just saying this because you stood up for me. I'm quick-tempered, I hit out without thinking. But I mustn't forget I'm in high school now. I ought to be ashamed. I'm not sure how to put this, but you have a quiet courage.

13

Mama is trying to shoo me off to bed. She's hoping to save herself trouble when it comes to waking me tomorrow morning. I can always read her mind. But since I'm on my best behavior it wouldn't do to be late for school. I'm sure you can wake up on time after a late night, but I just can't seem to manage it. So it's off to bed! Good night.

Naomi Niwa

Dear Setsuko,

Today is July 4. The Fourth of July is America's Independence Day. This commemorates the day America won its War of Independence and freed itself from British rule. I was taught the above by Mama. Before the war Mama and Papa had many American friends who invited them to their Fourth of July celebrations. Mama says she still regards them as her friends. Both my parents have a peculiarly stubborn streak. Papa was taken away by the police because of something called "thought." That was four years ago, and he still hasn't come back. Mama accuses him of being an unloving egotist, and says he could come home any time if he changed his "thought." And that if he really loved her, and me, there'd be no shame in that.

I don't understand these things very well, but I do know that when it comes to being an egotist, Mama's one too. Just listen to her calling our enemies, whose country is at war with us, her friends! I'm well aware that my Papa and Mama are altogether different from other people—too different for my liking. It's up to me, at least, to live as a true Japanese should, like you do.

I'm awfully glad, though, that you and I are both Japanese. Mama says you can't depend on two countries to stay on good terms. Japan and Germany might be allies now, but I learned from

14

her that in the First World War Japan fought on England's side against Germany. If we came from different places we might have to become enemies at the drop of a hat, whenever it suited our countries! Unbelievable! At the end of Les Thibault there's a part where the First World War has started and the boys of different nationalities who were living together in Switzerland go home to fight. Yesterday's friend is tomorrow's enemy, and Jacques is in despair.

I should make it clear, before going on, that the last part of Les Thibault isn't available in a book. Mama says they won't allow publication. We have it in French at home, and Mama translated it in exercise books. That's how I read it. Frankly, it's a pretty awful translation. Five pages of French boil down to a single page in Mama's notebooks. And she doesn't bother to look things up, either. But at least you can get the gist. Anyway, even the parts that have been published have lots of lines taken out, and it's often confusing. Mama is just lazy, really. It's no good expecting too much of her as a linguist, because Papa had to prod her along to the Athénée Français, and then it took years of lessons before she could read a book, more or less. It was Papa who ordered Les Thibault from Maruzen to begin with, she said, and he kept urging her to read it. But the first volumes of the translation came out straight away, so she didn't get around to reading the original for ages.

Then Papa was taken into custody and the book was banned before the last parts had been published, so she suddenly started to read it seriously. It's my guess that lazy old Mama only struggled through to the end because she missed Papa. She treasures the books of notes—I expect she wants Papa to praise her for them when he gets back.

I would so like you to read it, though, Setsuko.

Living alone with Mama, I gradually seem to be thinking quite *differently from other people. Lately I've realized just how different I've become. I must be more like you.*

We haven't had a letter from Papa for a while now. Sometimes I miss him so badly I can hardly bear it. But when I think how many children in Japan today are separated from their fathers, I know I'm being selfish. Children whose fathers are off fighting in the far south can't hope to see them, however much they're missed.

Is your brother well? All of my father's students have gone to the war, and I've heard that many of them have been killed already. The few postcards that come for Mama are either from someone leaving for the front, or news of another death—never one to say "I'm safely home." Do you suppose that none of Japan's soldiers ever comes back from the front?

I'm sorry. I didn't mean it. Mama's nonsense is affecting my brain. I promise I won't talk like that again. Well, goodbye for now. I'll see you very soon!

Naomi Niwa

Dear Setsuko,

At last! I'll be seeing you tomorrow. I won't sleep a wink tonight.

The end-of-term exams are just around the corner, but since we've had no proper classes there's nothing to worry about. Everyone has been more anxious about what will happen to the summer holidays this year. Then today the Morals teacher set us the Imperial Rescript Declaring War as a brush-writing assignment, so we concluded that if there's holiday homework there must be a holiday. That's a relief, but the very thought of writing out that long proclamation with a brush makes me feel quite faint. You can't erase mistakes, and you'd really catch it if you handed it in incorrect! What's the point of tormenting school pupils with such things in these hard times? I listen to myself grumbling and I think, "Aha, you're your mother's daughter, all right!" I'm sure you would get it letter-perfect from beginning to end. Memorizing it wouldn't have been so bad—I've got it down by heart already, because they said it might be in the entrance exam for high school. (It wasn't, though.)

Even when school gets out for the summer, I can't have fun with you, and I can't go to the beach, or the mountains, or the pool, so what good are holidays anyway? The only advantage is that I won't have to go to school and face Yoshiko Akiyama and the teachers every day, thank goodness. The part I hate most is when we write compositions on the eighth of every month for Imperial Rescript Day. Whether it's a letter to encourage a soldier at the front or an essay on labor service, I can't put the thought of Papa out of my head, and whatever I write my heart isn't in it. I tell myself that Papa is Papa, and I'm me. Though honestly I don't think I'm cut out to be the fine supporter of the war effort that you are, Setsuko. I don't know what to do about it.

No lessons and no summer holiday: can this be school life? If we go on neglecting our studies like this, and you go into the fourth-year class next year, do you suppose you'll have to graduate the following spring? To have your diploma and not have done the lessons would be very irregular. They should put us "on leave of absence."

We're not schoolgirls now—I'm a farmhand and you're a factory apprentice. I think we ought to be clearer about that in our minds. In this emergency, Japan needs us to produce rather than study. I think we should concentrate on working in earnest.

"We ought," "we should." What's wrong with me today? I'm not usually like this. This isn't the Naomi you know, is it? I can't stand being with Mama day in and day out. She's crazy. She loses

her temper on the slightest pretext, then she sheds great big tears and starts to wonder whether she could join Papa if she murdered someone. Unless Papa comes home very soon, I think Mama will go out of her mind. But you know, Setsuko, I'm only fourteen. I can't possibly take care of Mama. She's spoiled and selfish and not a bit motherly. Sometimes I truly hate her. How could anyone behave like that in a national crisis? I look at her and think of you, and count the days till I can see you. It's the only thing that keeps me going. And now it's tomorrow.

In the morning, I think I may greet the first rays of the sun with an inhuman yell!

Naomi Niwa

Setsuko slept some more. The dense memories surged over her weakened body like tidal waves, tiring her very easily. Then they burst into her sleep. The marching memories seemed quite orderly compared to the way that dreams barged in.

Blood streaming over pale skin. When Naomi hit Yoshiko Akiyama, she fell and put her hand through a glass cupboard door. The blood formed a little pool at her feet while they watched. No, it was coming from her neck, not her hand. Holding her, Setsuko staggered and fell under the weight. "Run, Ōizumi-san! Japan is surrounded by American warships," a hoarse, barely audible voice was warning her. It wasn't Yoshiko in her arms but Jun Sawabe. "Ōizumi-san, the war is ending. Save your own life."

"You mustn't die, Sawabe-san." Setsuko covered Jun Sawabe's wound with both hands, trying to stanch the flow, and wept aloud. However tightly she pressed her fingers together, blood welled up between them. Then it was her own mouth she was covering as the spurts of blood rose from her chest.

18

She was woken by a heaving cough. Turning from habit onto her side, she spat blood between her lips. She felt it wet her cheek and ear, and soak into her hair, while she almost fainted from the effort of breathing. Then another coughing fit brought her to her senses. The hemorrhage slowly subsided as this happened repeatedly. The smell of actual blood blended smoothly into the smell of blood in her dreams. Her dreams took just what they needed from reality and twisted it into their coil. Waking suddenly, Setsuko would carry a dream in all its sharp certainty into the darkness of actual time.

It hadn't been long since Setsuko first suspected she was ill. A cold she'd caught the previous winter had persisted, and the cough never left her. A routine checkup at the beginning of May had revealed trouble in her lungs and the doctor had advised her to leave the factory and return to school, as pupils in poor health were allowed to do. Setsuko had refused. Neither the doctor nor her teacher would overrule her wish to remain in the ranks where she could make some small contribution of her own. Death rained down on her in those days, and all were called upon to keep up the struggle with every last ounce of strength. Naomi and her mother were dead by then; they had died in April. In May it was her father, in June her mother; then Hajime's last postcard had come close behind. In July she'd been notified of Shōichi Wakui's death, and in August Jun Sawabe had died. During those lonely nights in the shelter among the debris, Setsuko was genuinely glad that by ignoring her illness she had taken the route toward death herself.

From August 15 on, she grew impatient at death's slowness. She wanted to rush to meet it. But, weak as she was, her body was young, and death drew near at its slackest pace. Since it was her lot to die last, Setsuko had been forced to face the deaths of many people dear to her, though only Jun Sawabe had slipped away from her very grasp. She hadn't found out about the fire bomb that killed Naomi and her Mama until a week after the event. Her father was, strictly speaking, missing, and her mother had died instantly in a strafing attack while on her way to draw rations, so that by the time Setsuko got home from the factory her body was cold. The deaths of her brother—a volunteer for the kamikaze squads—and of Shōichi Wakui had taken place so far away that her heart could not reach out to them. Only Jun Sawabe had died in Setsuko's arms, trying until the moment he lost consciousness to tell her something.

"Ōizumi-san, the war is ending. You must survive after coming this far. You're sick, and we've lost the war, and the American Combined Fleet has been off the coast at Kujūkuri for days now. They're negotiating our surrender at this moment, I *know* they are, because my father's in the Foreign Ministry. It doesn't matter how many more vacuum tubes you risk your life to make now. There's just no point."

In her dreams Setsuko clung tearfully to Sawabe, though in reality she'd hardly wept at all. He seemed to have said a great deal, and yet he must have been silenced in less than a minute after the shrapnel tore his carotid artery. Sawabe had been crippled by polio in infancy. Each time the factory was bombed the two of them were the last to get out, running from one air-raid shelter to the next looking for a spare place. At first Setsuko had been able to help him, but later it was he who half carried her to cover, in spite of his lame right leg. Setsuko was winded before she'd run ten yards.

When the bomb hit, Setsuko was flung down into an open shelter immediately in front of her as earth and sand struck the hood that covered her head and shoulders with the force of a landslide. Sawabe's body toppled directly after her. If it hadn't been for his air-raid hood with its thick cotton padding, his head would have rolled like a convict's on the executioner's block. In the same moment, as his weight forced them down in a heap, Setsuko covered his neck wound with the palm of her hand. As she strained to catch his last words, she was staring at the warm red that overflowed between her fingers. Sawabe had disapproved of her reckless disregard for her own life and had often tried to persuade her that when one fell ill it was one's first duty to get better, no matter what was going on in the world at large. Setsuko would reply with a weak smile; and when Jun Sawabe's head lolled forward, only the shadow of an expression passed over her face. His death wasn't a parting. She would take the same road herself, very soon. He'd merely gone ahead and would be waiting for her just around the first turning.

Even then Setsuko couldn't conceive of surrender, however close to the truth Sawabe's last words might have been. She knew Japan wasn't winning. But defeat and surrender weren't the same thing. They might be beaten, but they would never surrender. They would fight till the last man, woman and child had fallen. Wasn't that why, each time there was news of a Glorious Sacrifice—Attu, Saipan, Okinawa—they had sworn with ever-deeper conviction to defend their homeland against invasion? So Setsuko had been taught, had believed, had lived. How could they possibly surrender in shame before the enemy had even set foot on their home ground? After Sawabe stopped breathing his mouth stayed slightly open, making his face appear surprisingly childish. Setsuko shed a tear or two as she laid a finger on his silenced lips and gently closed them.

When the all clear sounded, Setsuko spread out one of the pieces of newspaper she was carrying instead of tissue paper, and lowered Jun Sawabe's head onto it. Then she covered his face with a white square of artificial silk, a special-issue item for bombed-out families. And then she went slowly back to her workplace, alone. She stopped at the washbasin to rinse the blood from her hands and drink a little water.

"Mr. Sawabe of Section Three has died in action." When she reported in a quiet, dry voice, keeping her eyes lowered, a hollowness rang through the plant where the machines were starting up. Only the rumble of motors crossed the space with its usual precision, while the conveyor belt rolled on slowly and impassively between momentarily arrested hands.

"Where?"

"When?"

"A short time ago. In the first shelter from the gate, the one with no roof."

People ran outside, and Setsuko sat down at her workbench. Her job was welding the filaments of vacuum tubes. Today the fine tweezers looked very, very sharp as she picked them up. A fearful, indescribable weariness was pressing down on her. The weight that had knocked her down when Sawabe fell was still heavy on her shoulders. Setsuko placed her elbows on the bench, cupped her forehead in her hands, and shut her eyes. Shafts of light clashed behind her lids, and when the dazzle faded she caught a smell of blood on her fingers that washing had not removed. She remembered the color of Sawabe's blood pouring between them. She had applied all her strength to the wound, but his life had spilled out pitilessly between her fingers. As the smell of blood hung there in the darkness, Setsuko prayed there'd be no surrender. Not now.

The others returned to the factory floor to find Setsuko calmly at work. "Ōizumi-san, how can you be so calm!" Nobuko Akiyama's eyes were very red. "After Sawabe-san was always so good to you!"

Setsuko raised her eyes dully and gazed at her, then at the people gathered behind her, then slowly down at the bench. "There's a war on," she said. "That's how it is when there's a war on." Her voice tailed away as if she were talking to herself. There was no way she could let the others know the sadness behind her dry eyes. The one thing that kept her going was the certainty that she too would soon be dead—she had pinned everything on that. The merest hint of a smile flickered over her face.

"I never thought I'd hear *you* talk like that! That's traitor's talk!" Nobuko Akiyama gave Setsuko a hard look. It was August 13.

22

Though Setsuko could not have known it, the Emperor would declare an end to the war two days later.

"You're a disgrace to Hatono Girls' High. I'm ashamed to tell my father I've got a traitor's daughter in my class, that I go to school with the daughter of a spy who was caught by the police." Yoshiko Akiyama's shrill voice echoed around a corner of the corridor.

"Papa knows what he's doing! He says it's very important to stand up for your beliefs." Naomi's thin but clear voice answered firmly.

"In a crisis like this, your individualism is unpatriotic! If you talk like that, the police ought to take you away too!"

There was a short muffled exchange before Naomi suddenly struck Yoshiko on the cheek. Setsuko and the other weekly monitors, on their rounds to inspect the classrooms for tidiness, sensed something was going on and ran around the corner just in time to see Yoshiko stagger back against a wall bookcase, her hand breaking the glass front. Although the glass shattered violently, she got off with little worse than a scratch on the back of her hand. There were several trickles of blood, though, and the watching pupils turned pale with fright. Setsuko left the others to clean up the broken glass while she helped Yoshiko to the infirmary. The school nurse stopped the bleeding, applied disinfectant and mercurochrome, then carefully bandaged the hand and put it in a sling. Her meticulous care suggested the kind of special attention required not by the injury itself but by Yoshiko Akiyama. "It's lucky it wasn't a bad cut," Setsuko said, and meant it; but behind her words there was also concern for Naomi Niwa.

The Akiyamas' father was a major general in the army. There were few daughters of the military at Hatono Girls' High, a private school with Buddhist affiliations. He was away at the Indochinese front, but the previous year he had attended the school ceremony on Em-

23

pire Day, in uniform, and addressed the assembly before the headmaster gave his moral instruction. Both teachers and pupils treated the Akiyama sisters with special respect. Naomi was another special case, in her own way. After passing the entrance exam for a municipal girls' school in Shibuya, near where she lived, she had been refused admission. The problem was of course her father, imprisoned for ideological crimes. The headmaster at Hatono was a religious man, and an old school friend of Naomi's grandfather on her mother's side; thus, while fully aware of her special background, he had allowed her to take a vacant place at his school. Some of the teachers opposed her entry, but the others (many of them members of the priesthood) had backed the headmaster in the end, and Naomi had scraped through. But once in she could hardly have enjoyed her schooldays. She set her thin shoulders resolutely—cockily, even—as she endured her lonely life. Hatono was a regular five-year girls' high school; those who would normally be in the fifth year, however, had had their graduation brought forward from spring to fall under the Essentials of Reduced Middle and High School Attendance Requirements, while the fourth-year students had been mobilized for factory labor, so that Setsuko was already a senior in her third year. And her class was also due to be sent to a factory in neighboring Kawasaki at the end of May—just over a month away when the incident in the corridor happened. Setsuko was in the same class as Nobuko, the elder Akiyama sister, and thus had heard about Naomi right from the start, but she had never sided with those who frowned on Naomi's parentage. For some of the concepts in the Buddhist instruction she'd received since entering Hatono had stayed with her and grown, though perhaps they didn't amount to actual faith. Whatever his crime, the penitent criminal would be redeemed by Buddha's mercy. And besides, if the headmaster had seen fit to admit Naomi in full knowledge of her background, then it wasn't the pupils' place to criticize.

What's more, she really didn't want to spoil her happy memories of the school she was about to leave. And so Setsuko was greatly relieved when the cut proved not to be serious. After Yoshiko had been escorted home by her sister (both of them ignoring pale, tearful, apologetic Naomi), Setsuko returned to her classroom, entered "Nothing to report" in the monitors' daybook, and took it to the staff room. But she was unprepared for the scene she found there. Naomi, surrounded by a number of teachers, was staring stiffly at a point on the floor. No one spoke. Setsuko presented the daybook to Mr. Okimura, the duty teacher for the day, who was sitting with his back to the room and a thick English book open before him. He glanced over the page she held out and commented "Nothing to report, eh?" Running a hand through his graying hair, he twisted the corners of his mouth somewhat ironically. Mr. Okimura taught Japanese now, but in her first year Setsuko had had him for English. He often used to digress from the textbook to talk about the lives of the Brontës, for example, and it was characteristic of him to be immersed now in an English book, in full view of his colleagues, even though English was in disfavor as the enemy language. He glanced in Naomi's direction, moving only his eyes, and lowered his voice. "You know what happened, don't you?"

"Yes, sir."

"We may not have heard the last of this."

At that moment, Naomi was summoned to the headmaster's office under escort by the nurse, the head teacher and her homeroom teacher.

"You seem to have something to say."

"Yes, sir. I think it's wrong for people to make remarks now. Her enrollment was approved by the headmaster, and I think the teachers should have discouraged remarks right from the start."

From a teacher's point of view Setsuko Ōizumi was an ideal pupil: quiet, industrious, punctual, and pleasant too. Her choice of words had been mild enough—and yet this was clearly criticism of the teaching staff. Okimura stared at Setsuko, seeing her in a new light. Then he picked up his large seal from the pen tray, inked it carefully, and applied it firmly in the column headed "Inspected."

There was no official suspension. Naomi was told to remain away from school for several days, and the monitors were questioned by the headmaster as witnesses to the incident. The others simply recounted the facts, but Setsuko went further. In front of the astonished headmaster, head teacher and other staff, she repeated her view of Naomi's situation. She also went to see Naomi and accompanied her to the Akiyamas' house to apologize. As an old classmate of Nobuko's, Setsuko was known to the girls' mother, yet Mrs. Akiyama's expression never softened for a moment. She glared hatred not only for the culprit who had injured her dear daughter, but for Naomi's father as well. To Setsuko this was unfair, but Naomi was doubly hurt. Away from the house, Setsuko raised her head and said cheerfully, "We've done what we could. Let's not brood about it any more."

July –

Dear Naomi,

Thank you for the gray notebook. I've read your entries in it over and over. You write so well—such freely flowing thoughts. I expect it's because you read such a lot, but that's not the only reason. You also have a lively mind. Not like me. Composition was always my worst subject at school.

The books you brought last Sunday are in a pile on my desk: Daddy Longlegs, The Rose Lives, How Will You Live Your Life? and Les Thibault. As I haven't read many novels, I must confess I'm a little dismayed. I often wonder whether I'm worthy of your friendship. But I do love hearing you talk. I'll try my hardest to read the books too. I hope you'll be patient.

After all, I leave for the factory early in the morning and get home at night to a house blacked out because of air-raid warnings. On nights when there's no blackout I try to put in a little work at my schoolbooks. I don't agree that a student who does no lessons is not a student. I may have been drafted to a factory, but I'm a student still, and I'll do every little bit of study that I can squeeze in. I try to spend at least half an hour on each of math, science, Japanese and history. I use the reference books left over from my brother's exams. I hate to have to stop when the sirens go, but I manage as well as I can. If we're to win in a long war, it really is important for students to keep up their studies.

This morning I got up early to pollinate the pumpkins. We've trained a vine over the shelter in the yard and there are seven pumpkins on it already. The yellow flowers are quite beautiful. I gathered some of the loose petals after I'd finished, and have them floating in a jar of water on my desk. They've already wilted, but they've kept the same beautiful yellow color. I know you brought me this notebook last Sunday and that I'm to bring it back next Sunday. If I don't put something down today, two whole weeks will go by before I've written a word, and won't you be cross!

At first, working the treadle on my welding machine took all my concentration, but I've finally grown accustomed to factory life. There are more steps to making a vacuum tube than I'd ever have guessed, and mine is a very small part of the process. But it's not to be sneezed at, because there'd be no vacuum tube without it. It's the same as the relationship between the nation and the people. It brings home to me that as a member of the Japanese nation I am playing a part in the sacred war for our ideal of a Greater East Asia Co-prosperity Sphere. I was originally assigned to clerical duties,

27

but I asked for a transfer because it was so important to me to do actual factory work, and I'm glad I did. Some people on the shop floor envy the office workers—perhaps because it's a smaller group and they don't sit at workbenches all day as we do. Perhaps it looks like they're having a good time. But I don't think those who are envious fully appreciate the importance of our work.

Here's my impression of you when we met the other day: you have changed completely—but I wish you hadn't. I think I understand why you're on your best behavior at school, and I suppose I ought to praise you for showing such an improvement, but please don't force yourself to change too much. Please, at least when you're with me, be the same bright Naomi who chats about everything under the sun. You and I have grown up in different environments, we have different lives, and we also think differently—yet in spite of all these differences I'm sure we can be the best of friends. One day we may come to share the same ideas, but I'd like to believe that it's a natural growing together.

I've got to the end of La belle saison in Les Thibault. There are a lot of cuts in this volume, aren't there?—though I'm not sure I'd understand half of what it says even if it was uncut. It was all I could do to understand Le cahier gris and Le pénitencier. I can hardly believe that you read the book before you were twelve.

How different the French are from the Japanese—their way of thinking, and family love, and friendships, too. Look at how Jacques fights with his father. My father was a taxi driver before he was drafted to work at Nippon Aircraft. He left school after the sixth grade, and he's had a hard life. Once my brother entered middle school there was never a quarrel between them. After a cup or two of saké my father would go red in the face and tell his story: how he was class captain in every year of his country school, how he hoped to go on to high school but had to be apprenticed in the end, how he couldn't stifle his longing to study, and so he ran away from his master to the city in the hope of putting himself through night school. The story always ended with "You must finish school, whatever you do." When my brother took engineering, Father was overjoyed. Later, when he left to join the navy after all the work it had taken to get in, my father didn't try to stop him. But he never again said "You must finish school," even when he'd been drinking.

I can't imagine a father and son loving or hating as fiercely as Monsieur Thibault and Jacques do. And the same goes for religion: I can't understand all that feuding between Catholics and Protestants, when they're all Christians. I don't understand Antoine and Rachel, either. I'm sorry, Naomi. Do you know, I'm almost ashamed to admit how little I understand? I can only trot out the same old excuse: that I've read very few novels till now. But one thing I can tell you: I think I'm getting to like reading— though that's a bit scary.

The only religion I know is Buddhism. I still remember when we did the Shushōgi in my first year. My favorite bit goes: "Praise the man of virtue, pity the virtueless man. Let loving words lie at the source when a sworn enemy's hatred is overcome or wise men are reconciled. Kind words heard face to face bring gladness of heart; kind words spoken in one's absence are engraved upon heart and soul. Know ye that the power of loving words can move heaven and earth."

I'm looking forward to seeing you again.

Setsuko Ōizumi

Setsuko's thirst worsened beyond endurance. She decided she'd rather die going for water than die of thirst. Her eyes could see nothing but blackness however wide she opened them, but she could sense the night air, which had a cool touch of autumn to it. Insects chirruped above her head. Where had they sheltered when even the earth was seared to red dust? The fragile wisps of sound had filled Setsuko with amazement each night that she'd lain unable to rise since the Student Corps was disbanded on August 16. It seemed a near miracle: there were insects alive in the patches of weed on discolored, shriveled soil between gutted buildings. The insects were alive! Alive!

Fine green lines like rays of light floated in her darkness—as fine as silk threads, yet sparkling with the fresh green of life.

"Setchan, tomorrow I'm going to clear up what's left of the house. Can you give me a hand before you go in the morning?"

It was mid-June when her mother asked her to help. After losing their home in the May 29 raid, Setsuko and her mother had been living in one of the less damaged cars of a Keihin Express train on a siding of Yokohama Station, which they shared with several neighbors' families. For nearly two weeks they'd got by as best they could with the few items of food and clothing that Setsuko's mother had saved, the emergency supplies that had come through safely under the floor, and the special rations they drew as air-raid victims. During that time Setsuko went calmly to work at the factory while her mother searched all day for her missing father. He'd been coming down with a cold on the morning of the raid, and had set off for work a little later than usual. The air-raid sirens were already sounding, and Setsuko's mother had very nearly suggested that he stay home for the day. "It was on the tip of my tongue, but I stopped myself," she appealed again and again to Setsuko in a voice torn between grief and anger. Their prayers gave way to despair after two or three days of awaiting his return, and Setsuko's mother then set out early each morning and searched until dusk, hoping at least to find his remains. She went out day after day, even when the dead had been buried everywhere in temporary graves. Night after night Setsuko watched in silence as her mother huddled in a corner of a seat, her head covered with one of the rough earth-colored blankets supplied to the homeless, too tired to speak. Though she'd noticed that she too was tiring easily, Setsuko would light a fire in the small stove they'd salvaged, using scrap wood from their house, and persuade her mother to eat the rice broth or dumpling soup she made. On the first Sunday morning Setsuko rose early and, having first rinsed out the sweat-stained underwear she'd worn all week and hung it up to dry, offered: "I'll go with you today. How far have you searched?" Her mother shook her head forlornly. It wasn't easy to tell where her eyes were resting as she gazed vaguely out of a broken window. Those households that had enough able-bodied members and sufficient materials had already cleared their sites and begun to put up makeshift huts, while other families who'd been barely hanging on in the city had finally given up and evacuated to the country. The railway car, which had bustled with a strange kind of cheerfulness, now housed only Setsuko and her mother.

"Setchan, to tell the truth, I wasn't looking very hard. At first I meant to keep searching along the Keihin Express Line all the way to Nippon Aircraft in Sugita. But after a while I couldn't go on picking over one pile of charred corpses after another, lifting them one by one to see if I recognized them. It made me sort of breathless and dizzy. In the worst places, you couldn't even tell men from women. And when I thought about each of these people having a family, and having managed to stay alive till now, I hadn't the heart to go on turning them over and opening up their mouths for a look inside and all the time not caring about anyone except your father. I guess I give up too easily. Other people are still out there searching. They haven't given up. You know that road up the hill from Kogane-chō Station going toward Kantō College? That's as far as I got. Then I got stuck, I just couldn't keep moving. I sat among the dead with my eyes closed as if I was one of them myself. I wondered if that mightn't be your father beside me for all I knew. And even after the bodies were cleared away I went back and sat there every day. It comes to the same thing. Whether it was him or not, it was all the same to me."

But that day, with her mother as a reluctant guide, Setsuko traced the route she'd taken among the remains. The piles of bodies she'd described were gone, and Setsuko was accustomed by now to the rubble that stretched as far as the eye could see. It was where she herself lived. The terrible black smoke that had obscured the sun and turned day to night had gone, and a few families had patched together places just big enough to huddle in, from posts and foundation stones and roofing iron, like bagworms encasing themselves in scraps of dead leaf. Setsuko stood for a long time on the slope where her mother had sat day after day. When she closed her eyes her father moved back and forth across turbid space, appearing as she'd known him at different times in the past. Feeding his goldfish, which were almost too big for the tiny pond in the tiny garden; celebrating the summer festival with the neighborhood children as they paraded their miniature shrine, wearing a cotton kimono that matched theirs, its hem tucked up and a polka-dotted towel knotted around his forehead; tending pots of morning glories for the big flowers he loved so. Oddly, all the scenes were in summertime. As he couldn't stand the cold, Setsuko thought of him snug in the *kotatsu* all winter long. Her mother's words came back to her: It comes to the same thing. Whether it was him or not, it was all the same to me. Every one of the dead in those charred heaps had had a life. Setsuko felt the weight of memories that only their families would know added to those of her own father. Then she set her gaze, blurred by tears, on the desolate, razed city, and while taking it in with her whole body she repeated deep inside the words she'd often murmured before: That's the way it is when there's a war on. Her mother went out the next day, apparently, and the day after that, but before long she stopped and began to talk of clearing the wreckage of their house. It had taken more than two weeks for her husband's death to sink in; Setsuko thought it a long time, and then again surprisingly short.

That morning, under a sky hazy with the onset of the June rains, Setsuko and her mother worked together to raise a sooty sheet of iron. The blackness of the earth beneath startled them. Along the edge of a foundation stone stood several strands of bright yellow-green, like lengths of silk thread set out in a row. Grass shoots: etiolated and feeble, but undeniably grass shoots. Mother and daughter both went down on their knees to touch the green. The next moment Setsuko's mother put her face in her hands as she knelt there, and quiet sobs escaped between her fingers for a time. Watching, Setsuko thought of her father's life which would not return.

Now, as she listened to the insects sing in the darkness, she thought of the hardy weeds that gave them shelter. Neither grass nor insects had any part in the war. That was why they had been allowed to come back to life. But not people. The people who had made war would never come back. For hadn't the war taken the lives even of its opponents like Naomi's father and Shōichi Wakui? Setsuko strained to hear the footsteps of her own approaching death. And saw again, in the insects' singing, the green shoots like silk threads.

"Come and join in, Ōizumi-san." The ball was as white as the clouds it flew toward in a blue sky. The students were playing with a volleyball in their lunch break, tossing it in a circle of boys and girls together. Setsuko just looked on and smiled. Under school rules they would normally have been wearing black or dark jackets, but on the factory floor and during breaks they were allowed to go in shirt sleeves. It was almost summer. The coastal belt between Yokohama and Tokyo had been virtually reduced to a wasteland and the air raids came less frequently. It was now the cities of the provinces that were steeped nightly in hellfire.

Setsuko leaned against a wall and watched her classmates' lively movements. She had no uniform for the summer. Most of the clothes her mother had saved, either burying them beneath the floor or storing them in the shelter, had been their best things. She'd carefully laid away the kimonos of her youth, fearing they could never be replaced; but what Setsuko needed now was a white cotton short-sleeved blouse. She couldn't have played volleyball, though, even if she'd had one; just standing and watching in her loose serge pants and jacket, she was perspiring heavily. Yet as she followed the play from the sidelines Setsuko didn't feel entirely left out, for Jun Sawabe was watching too, from the shade of a phoenix tree a little way off. No one asked him to join in because they knew about his bad leg, but when the ball rolled toward him he picked it up and tossed it back athletically. Until her cough and shortness of breath had forced her to drop out a few months earlier, Setsuko had been in the game herself, while Sawabe had always watched silently.

Setsuko followed the white ball with her eyes and smiled when the players laughed, but she knew very well it wasn't the volleyball game that brought her there. The knowledge made her almost tremble with shame and the fear of discovery. But she stayed very still despite her secret agitation, and kept her eyes on the straggly circle which always re-formed just when it seemed about to dissolve. Out of the corner of her eye, meanwhile, she never lost sight of the motionless figure in the black student uniform.

Dear Setsuko,
Have you seen the newspaper?
"Paris Falls."

*I have very mixed feelings. Properly speaking I should be sad-
dened and vexed by the fact that our German allies are losing. But
I'm not. I know how happy the people of Paris must be. Jacques
and Jenny may only be characters in a novel, but they're more
than that to me. I don't think even you, Setsuko, could understand
how eagerly I read* Les Thibault. *They were my special friends
when I was all alone. And so their beloved Paris is a special place
for me, too.*

*The papers said, "Paris Falls," but I wouldn't call it that. Paris
fell when the Germans invaded. It just collapsed. The teachers
and girls at school said it showed Germany's power and France's
weakness. When I came home and repeated that to Mama, she said
it was quite typical of Paris, that Paris has a history of falling
before invasions that goes back to the Hundred Years' War, but
every war comes to an end and when peace is restored Paris rises
like a phoenix. War has never finished Paris, she said. I was too
small to understand properly at the time, but I've remembered
what she said and kept thinking about it, and now I believe I do
understand.*

*Knowing you, Setsuko, has made me want to live more like a
true Japanese should and to think in a truly Japanese way. I have
been trying, you know. I've always considered myself to be quite
unlike Mama, but I had to examine my own feelings today when I
saw her excitement over the headlines. She said, "See, I told you.
The bad times are coming to an end." I'm quite sure you were
upset by the news, Setsuko. But as I've said before, you and I are
different. The thought of how very different we are has made me
feel gloomy all day. I'm still not up to the mark. And I'm afraid
that no matter how hard I try I may never succeed in dedicating
myself to victory and living as a Japanese should, as you do,
Setsuko.*

Setsuko, do you think that war is different for the French? They say there were many women and children on Saipan, and they all refused to surrender. But not the people of Paris. Do you suppose the Germans occupying Paris all fought to the death? Or is it only we Japanese with our Yamato spirit who would rather die than surrender? Mama got awfully angry over the newspaper editorial that said the Glorious Sacrifice on Saipan means that the American occupiers can build airfields there and use them to launch massive air raids on Japan, because it said that once the war is waged on the Japanese mainland we'll fight to the end and decide the outcome on our own ground. Insanity, Mama called it. According to her, anyone who truly believes that the Japanese will fight to the last man, woman and child must be out of his mind.

I don't know. Maybe it's Mama who's out of her mind.

I'm in horrible despair. Perhaps Jacques felt like this after his attempt to distribute leaflets from Meynestrel's airplane ended in failure. I've despaired of ever becoming a fine daughter of Japan like you, Setsuko. I can't forgive myself—I was actually relieved that our friends the Germans are falling back and the Allied Army is rapidly gaining ground. I've tried, but I can't feel sorry to see Paris belonging to the Parisians again.

Naomi

Dear Setsuko,

It's a very hot night. The heat's getting me down, and to make matters worse Mama got into a dreadfully bad mood today. I wanted to cry, and I was on the point of running away from home. I remembered how Jacques and Daniel ran away and wandered the streets of Marseilles. But since all the bakeries have closed and you can't even get meal coupons to eat in restaurants unless you've got *a rice ration book, it's not too easy to run away these days! What a laugh! Though it's kind of sad, too.*

Earlier today, Grandmother came over from Ōmori—we hadn't seen her for ages. My Ōmori grandmother is Mama's mother. As Mama was the youngest, and the only girl, she was very pampered. But since Papa's arrest she hasn't been on speaking terms with my Ōmori grandfather. In fact even Grandmother hardly ever writes, for fear of what Grandfather would say. Then today she tried to persuade Mama to go along with them when they evacuate to Suwa in Nagano Prefecture. Not actually to live with them, though—she offered to rent another house nearby, and keep it a secret. Grandfather owns a factory that makes machine parts and it's supplying some special invention of his to the army, so he associates with a lot of the top brass, and because of that Mama can't go back to the house where she was born. The army has ordered the whole factory to evacuate to Suwa, you see. Well, Mama refused, so Grandmother's visit had to end in saying good-bye. As she left, in tears, she said Mama was making it hard on me, too, by her own selfishness. This seemed to me very ironic. Yes, I have had a hard time because of her selfishness, but not at all in the way that Grandmother meant. Mama loves Papa. And so do I. (He really is wonderful. It's such a pity I can't introduce you!) I'm sorry to say that Grandfather just can't hold a candle to Papa. And that's why Mama won't get a divorce or even leave the house she once shared with Papa. Grandfather is really a very nice man, if it weren't for the fuss about Papa. He's the one who's always come to the rescue—he saw that I was admitted to Hato-no when I couldn't get into the local girls' high, and he's been sending checks to Mama all the time that Papa's been away. And if we had evacuated with them, I expect that the business about not telling Grandfather would only have been to keep up ap-

pearances—he probably knew all along. These aren't the things that make it hard on me.

After Grandmother left, Mama started drinking that strong liquor called shōchū. She's friendly with a dealer on the black market, and we've got masses of things in the house that can be traded for shōchū or food. Grandmother had a ridiculous number of kimonos made for Mama's trousseau, since she was the only girl in the family, but since her marriage Mama has worn only Western clothes. The storeroom is full of kimonos she's never even put on. Mama laughs and says, "I never thought we'd be eating those kimonos one day!"

At first she drank quietly and sang "When the Violet Blooms," but as she got drunker and drunker she started to say things like "Why did I ever fall in love with a man like your Papa?" and "He can drop dead for all I care!" And she ended up screaming "Ah, I'm fed up with this war!" Then she was sick, and turned white as a sheet, and began to cry. Before she fell asleep, though, she mumbled "I'm sorry, Naomi dear."

Please help me, Setsuko. I can't stand it any more.

> *Naomi*

> *September –*

Dear Setsuko,

When I got up this morning, surprise, surprise! Mama, in an apron, was cleaning the house. There was no sign of the mess in the dining room from the night before, and on the table was a fancy school lunch. Mama had woken at 3:30 and been hard at work ever since. She said she had a terrible hangover, and she did look pale. She smiled sadly and said "Naomi, my sweet, I'm sorry. I know I've been behaving badly." I hardly knew what to say.

Then, over breakfast, Mama suggested I should go with Grand-mother to Suwa. She said she didn't want to leave our house, but that I was still young, with my own life to live, and I didn't have to follow in the footsteps of my Papa or Mama.

I asked for some time to think and we dropped the subject. I've been thinking about it all day, until I realized that I was being a complete individualist.

A quiet life with Grandmother and Grandfather does seem very nice compared to being driven crazy by Mama day after day—but then the thought of being separated from you got in the way. Also, I thought, if Papa came home Mama would see him before I did, which doesn't seem fair. But once I realized that all of this was nothing but individualism, I made up my mind. I won't go to Suwa, for the simple reason that we're about to be mobilized to a drug factory in Kamata. The time has come when even I can serve my country. Thinking of you, and knowing that in my place you'd never dream of going to the country, I knew at once what I should do.

It did make me think about destiny, though, Setsuko. If I'd been born a year later, I'd have been evacuated already like all the sixth graders. I'd have had no choice. Just a year's difference can affect a person's destiny—or even a day's, or an hour's.

But when it comes to the point, I wonder if I'll be able to work. That's what worries me. Mama has never believed I could do it, and I don't blame her. I wonder what it's like? Do you remember when I asked you, ages ago? You said, "You could call it hard, or you could call it easy. You could even say it's hard because it's so easy." I'd never heard you speak in such riddles before, and I knew then that I couldn't imagine it, that it defied the imagination. (I'm reading Tales of the Antarctic Explorers. *Lieutenant Shirase and Amundsen and Scott all went through hardships that defy the imagination.)*

Anyway, I feel much better now that I've made up my mind. Please forgive poor Mama. I'll do her share for the country. I'll work as hard as a regular factory hand. I'm going to read The Girl from the Brickworks *by Fumiko Nozawa again.*

Setsuko, I've got no one but you to turn to. Please be kind to me.

Naomi Niwa

For quite some time, several mosquitoes had been whining close to Setsuko's ear. When one landed on her cheek she would twitch it away, but still they hung nearby, settling now on her ear, now on the nape of her neck. It was a surprise to find that she instinctively flinched from their attacks even now: what reason did she have to fend them off when, lying covered in blood, mud and sweat, she was reduced to a sickening clot of foul smells? Or so she appeared to herself, there in the darkness, as she stretched her free hand into space and wiggled her fingers at the mosquitoes. Her skin seemed to have taken over the power of sight.

The mosquitoes stayed airborne, sometimes touching Setsuko's skin but taking fright at the tiniest movement. The lice were far more brazen. Setsuko thought their fatness unfair, considering the wasted condition of the body they were battening on. She stared in the dark at the rows of white eggs that she knew would be lining the seams of her underwear, which she'd had on for days now. The impossibly swollen eggs began to heave, then hatched out more lice, and these in turn laid eggs which hatched again. Setsuko could feel her body swarming with them. They'll be out of luck when I die, she thought. She put her hand inside the breast of her jacket and let it travel over her slippery skin till it met a small, flat bump which skidded out at once from under the ball of her finger. She could see the little white shape scuttling away on its many short, thin legs.

40

"You shouldn't get too friendly with Yoshida-san," Nobuko Akiyama had whispered. Her big round eyes glinted with the secret: "Yoshida-san has lice. You'll catch them too if you're friendly with her." Setsuko looked in astonishment from Nobuko to Asako Yoshida, who as usual seemed somehow left out. She was an extremely quiet girl, the only farmer's daughter in the class. This was at the beginning of the war, before it had affected their living conditions. Of course, a farmer's family affluent enough to send a daughter to high school would not live in lice-breeding squalor, and yet she did look countrified among all these city girls. They kept up a veneer of friendship toward Asako while deftly avoiding her. Having just entered high school that spring, the girls may have wanted to establish themselves as special in some way.

Three years later, as Setsuko sat behind Nobuko at morning assembly, what did she spy running in and out of her braided hair? Lice spread easily from head to head as the girls rode to the factory in trains so crowded that a window sometimes shattered. As Nobuko's father was a career officer they shouldn't have lacked clothing or soap, yet it was extremely difficult to get rid of the vermin once one had picked them up. Asako brought white rice in her lunch box every day, and presents of fresh farm eggs for the teachers and the foreman. She had many pairs of work pants and silk serge jackets, always neatly pressed, and in winter she wore a good heavy overcoat. But Setsuko had seen them: rows of tiny eggs in a lock of Asako's hair straying in the breeze.

After the fire, Setsuko had suddenly found lice not only in her hair but on her body too. The head lice were black, the body lice white. Her mother had frantically boiled their clothes in a washbasin, but as they had no bath and few changes of clothing the lice multiplied faster than they could be destroyed.

I wonder what the lice will do when I die? In the darkness Setsuko saw an agitated formation departing her dead body. They swelled to

41

infinite size, white and sleek and round. No sooner had they abandoned her than Setsuko turned to bare bones which crumbled soundlessly to ash and sank into the dark earth as into a bottomless mire.

Dear Naomi,

Thank you for all the treats you brought today. I'd quite forgotten what bean-jam dumplings taste like when they're made with real sugar. And seaweed wafers, and dried sardine paste—all of Father's favorites. He's just come home with a special saké ration from the factory, and he's looking very contented tonight.

But, Naomi, listen. If you'd been stopped in the street with all these things on you, you'd have been in deep trouble. Please don't take risks like that again. I can't offer you anything in return, and besides—I don't quite know how to say this, but—I feel uncomfortable about it. I can't get over the feeling that I'm doing something wrong. Of course, Father and I couldn't serve the nation adequately if we ate only rations, and sometimes I do go to bargain for farm produce on my day off. But I try to go only when absolutely necessary. I hope you'll understand. It's very painful having to refuse your kindness, but I believe you will understand. Would you kindly pass on my request to your mother?

Hatono High has been joined at the factory by girls' schools from Tokyo and Kawasaki. The girls from Satomi High School who work in our section still wear their proper woolen jackets and well-made navy-blue serge trousers with black socks and leather shoes. When they start work they put on aprons of floral print with frilly borders, and afterward they wash their hands with soap that smells nice. When we receive a special ration of vegetable and rice gruel, they give theirs away to the apprentices.

I'm amazed at how well supplied they are. Those things

couldn't possibly have been distributed officially, so either their families have been hoarding or they're using the black market. And yet they don't appear the least bit ashamed. In fact they're the envy of all the others who don't have such luxuries, who wear patched rayon clothes and battered shoes, when you'd think they would despise them instead. A friend of mine who's chummy with a Satomi girl was invited to her birthday party, and they had a feast of ceremonial rice with red beans and Western cakes. It's a fact that some people aren't going without, even in times like these—I'm not saying that you and your mother are the only ones.

But I don't want to be a part of it. When I think of the soldiers at the front, I just can't. Japan is in a state of emergency, and I want to be able to hold my head high as a Japanese at all times.

I've always felt this way, and that's why I can't accept your generosity. Please understand.

Setsuko Ōizumi

September –

Dear Naomi,

Remember you said you'd like to hear about my brother? I'm not a good talker, and when we're together I always let you do the talking. So today I'm going to write a bit about my brother.

Hajime Ōizumi

Age: 22

He was attending Tokyo Engineering School, but last December he volunteered as a naval cadet, was mobilized, and is now in the Kitaura Air Squadron.

He has a passion for trains, and if he could have fought in one he wouldn't be up in some old airplane. But trains on their fixed tracks are no use in battle.

43

We have a lot of model locomotives here that my brother made. Freight cars, too, which you can load with all kinds of goods and hitch together in a long line. The funny thing is that although the locomotives and cars are very realistic, the cutout figures that are supposed to be cattle could easily be pigs, or dogs, or horses, except that they have horns.

My brother dreamed that when he grew up and started earning money he would build a model as big as he could, with a genuine coal-fired engine sending out genuine puffs of smoke. He'd lay a track on some unused land. He'd ride the locomotive, and children could ride on the cars, and they'd go bowling merrily along. He's like a child himself. With the best will in the world I couldn't describe him as wonderful and handsome like your father, but I do love him.

Another thing he's good at is whistling. His favorite used to be "The Sky of My Hometown."* If I listen hard enough I can still hear it: "Oh, how clear the evening sky, How fresh the autumn breeze. Soft the moonbeams all about, And sweet the crickets' song." If I close my eyes I can see him whistling over a model train he's building.

He hates writing, though. Maybe it runs in the family, because composition is my worst subject too. It's nearly ten months since he went off to the war, and we've only had one postcard from him when he was transferred to Kitaura. It's really too bad of him, even if he does hate writing, and it's especially hard on Mother. I wrote and said so, but we still haven't had a letter. I give up. I think my brother is very rude and takes his family for granted.

He has a close friend called Shūzō Wakui. They've known each other since middle school and they went to Engineering School

---

*Japanese lyrics were set to the tune of "Comin' Through the Rye" in the 19th century, and later generations knew it only as a Japanese song. After being used in a popular wartime film, it came to symbolize the beauty of personal sorrow in war.

together. Both signed up last year and they're both at Kitaura now, though in different units. Mother and I went to see them this spring, just after you'd got into trouble, and I told them about the incident. To my surprise, Shūzō Wakui knew your father—not personally, but because his oldest brother was a student of his at the university and attended seminars at your house. Shūzō's brother was arrested a long time ago over an ideological problem, and they say he's ill. Apparently your father went to a lot of trouble at the time, trying to intercede with the police. Isn't it strange how people are connected? You never can tell.

Now I've told you my brother's dream, but when I ask myself what chance it has of ever coming true, I could cry. Antoine in Les Thibault *had grand dreams as a doctor, and he worked so hard to fulfill them, but the war destroyed everything in the end. Compared to that, it hardly matters if someone's dream of giving train rides to children on a grassy lot should come to nothing. But my brother, as I know him, is cut out more to be a train-ride driver than a fighter pilot. I've never said this to anyone before and I don't suppose I shall again. You're the only person I'll ever tell.*

Naomi, don't you think there's a certain way of life that's right for each of us? I couldn't hold back the tears as I read of Jacques' end. It takes true courage to act in the opposite way to everybody else. I don't understand what your father has done, but there's no need to persuade yourself that your parents are wicked. You love them, and that's what matters.

Setsuko Ōizumi

Setsuko returned to sharp reality. She'd been enduring her physical needs for quite some time; she'd have to struggle out of the shelter now, however laboriously, to relieve her thirst and her bladder. Groping, she shut the gray notebook up in the duffel bag which hung from one shoulder; the water flask was slung over the other, their straps crossing. Then she turned cautiously onto her side and paused to catch her breath, fighting back a cough. She lowered herself very gingerly till she lay face down, but still had to endure a paroxysm of coughing and gasping. Then she pushed up till she barely raised her body from the waist and began inching toward the exit. The roof was too low to stand upright anyway, but Setsuko doubted she'd have the strength to get to her feet once outside. She took two rests on the five steps, and at the top her body seemed so heavy that she looked back over her shoulder, scarcely believing it could be her own weight. Her panting brought on a shooting pain in her ears, and she was afraid of slipping down to the shelter floor, but somehow she did crawl out onto open ground where she lay inert for some time. The night breeze was cool on her hot cheeks, and after a while the breathlessness and the pain in her ears faded until they might never have existed. Setsuko lifted her head a little and opened her eyes. Stars shone in the deep distance with a beautiful light. For a moment she suspected her eyes were playing tricks, but they continued to shine just as beautifully as she stared and stared.

Then suddenly they swayed and their light blurred. Tears were tumbling over her lids and down her cheeks. She heard her brother's voice in the starry sky: "Haven't you finished yet? Hurry up!" He sounded cross. Setsuko chuckled aloud as the scene came back; the sudden memory brought both tears and laughter. Once, when she was little, she'd begged Hajime to take her to a night fair in the temple grounds, and on the way home announced she had to go to the bathroom. As her brother stood in helpless embarrassment—they were still a long way from home—she pleaded desperately "I can't hold on, I can't!" He made her squat in long grass while he waited at the side of the road, tapping his foot impatiently. "Aren't you finished yet? Hurry up!" The stars had been beautiful that night, too.

No one was looking. No one would even be awake. The privy was fifteen or twenty feet farther than the water tap. Untying her trousers at the waist, she slipped into the concealment of a clump of weeds behind the shelter.

"You read a lot, don't you?" The footsteps she'd expected to pass by had stopped beside Setsuko's workbench. "Do you like books?" Above ankle-length black boots, which although pigskin were at least new, the puttees were bound with admirable exactitude to just below the knees of the dark uniform trousers. Setsuko felt embarrassment flame instantly from her cheeks to her ears. It wasn't as if the other girls shunned the male students' company; but Setsuko herself was quite unused to such things. "What are you reading?" The boy's name was Kiyoshi Harada. (All the students had to wear a white cloth patch sewn to the breast of their uniforms, listing name, address, school, age and blood type.) He was a secret heartthrob of the girls, for he was tall and supposedly resembled the star of the movie *The Imperial Navy*.

"That's *Wuthering Heights*, isn't it?" He'd noticed the name Heathcliff on the open page. Setsuko was overcome with confusion. Not only had a popular boy suddenly spoken to her, but he had entirely the wrong idea about her. Her panic made her all the more tongue-tied.

"Er ... I ... don't like books," she hedged. But that wasn't the truth, either. Setsuko had come to like reading in the six months since Naomi first brought her a load of books which she'd tackled half-reluctantly (for reading novels was a form of idleness not encouraged in an ordinary household like hers). "Well, yes, I've taken to them recently, but I haven't read many. Only about fifteen."

At the precision of this figure, Harada laughed merrily. "What an interesting way of putting it!" Over his words, Setsuko could hear

Hajime's: "What a queer fish you are!" She was miserable. Why did he laugh, when it was true? The bell rang; lunch break was over. Harada said "Bye!" and ran up the stairs.

"What were you and Kiyoshi Harada talking about?" Atsuko Yokoyama knew all about the latest films and popular songs, and she kept a photo of the actor that Harada was supposed to resemble in the pocket of her train pass holder. Setsuko didn't much care for Atsuko, who sat next to her. She was always going off for a long chat with a friend at another bench, leaving two or three boxes backed up at her station on the production line.

"Oh, nothing much."

"You've got something to hide, by the look of it." That was what Setsuko disliked most about Atsuko. Feeling as though something nasty had been daubed on the back of her neck, Setsuko rubbed her jaw against her shoulder. Familiar footsteps were climbing the stairs: the first thumped firmly, the bannister creaked, then there was a heavy dragging step that came level with the first. The left foot moved up a step. The bannister creaked. The right foot was lifted and brought down beside the other. Jun Sawabe was such an unremarkable student that if it hadn't been for his leg he mightn't have come to anyone's attention at all. Initially, the only reason Setsuko had been conscious of his footsteps was that her bench was the closest to the stairs. Although he took a little longer to climb them, in every other respect he was just as capable as the other students. In fact, his work was clearly the most accurate in the inspection department. It wasn't his work that made him feel a burden to the others: it was the march-past on Imperial Rescript Day, the eighth of every month, when his paralyzed leg would cruelly exclude him from the ranks of the students parading in the square before the main building. He stood rigidly to attention throughout in an out-of-the-way corner of the grounds, not allowing himself to relax for a moment. It must have been very hard for him, both physically and mentally. No one would have objected if, for instance, he had stayed on the job instead of watching the drill; they might even have welcomed this solution, which would have provided him with a way of shouldering his own burden and working off his sense of unworthiness. But Sawabe wouldn't do that. Setsuko thought that in his place she would probably have done the same thing, and this gave her a secret respect for him—though as yet they'd never even said hello.

At three in the afternoon the loudspeakers played a popular song:

> Give of your best, your hidden power!
> Fall into step as we stride along,
> Men of the land where the cherries flower.
> Forward we march, a hundred million strong,
> Down the straight road of true loyalty.
> Invincible Army of the Rising Sun,
> Subjects of His Imperial Majesty,
> Come, forward march! We've just begun!

The door opened and the foreman dropped a crate with a thud. "Hey, special rations—frozen mandarins!" The regular workers made a dash for the doorway. There were no special rations for the students, though.

"How do you like that?" Atsuko and the others grumbled among themselves. "We're good industrial soldiers too, aren't we?"

Setsuko usually showed no interest, but just once, when Rising Sun headbands with the word "kamikaze" had been distributed to the factory hands, she had gone to the foreman and told him the students wanted them too. With the eyes of all the teachers and office staff on her, Setsuko had repeated clearly: "Please give us kamikaze headbands too!"

"There aren't any for the students."

"Why is that?"

"*Why?*" The foreman had turned his face away, unable to meet Setsuko's eyes. "Better not glare like that if you want to find a husband!" He gave a humorless laugh.

> Pure white Fuji's majesty
> Is their hearts' stout shield.
> The women who serve our country
> Are the mountain cherry blossoms
> Of this glorious reign,
> The flowers of the nation
> Spreading beauty o'er the land.

"Flowers of the Beloved Country" always closed the musical selection, perhaps because there were so many girls in the factory.

In the evening, around the time when a weary silence began to extend over the factory floor, the loudspeaker crackled again. The stirring "Battleship March" was followed by: "Here is an announcement from Imperial Headquarters. Our fleet is . . ." As Setsuko sat up straight and listened intently to the bulletin like the other girls, she felt her chest tighten. The greater the military gains, the higher the losses on our side. Until Hajime went off to the war she'd thought the losses praiseworthy, honorable, but now they secretly pained her. "The army and navy have combined in a fierce assault on the enemy task force and transport ships. Gains to hand are as follows: four aircraft carriers, two cruisers, one destroyer and at least four troopships have been sunk, and one carrier has been destroyed." Setsuko shut her eyes. What price must we have paid in losses for such a great toll? "Casualties on our side are: two cruisers and one destroyer sunk. Aircraft not returned . . ." When would Hajime's be one of them? They gave statistics of ships and planes, but Setsuko's pain was at the thought of the lives that those sunken vessels and lost planes represented. She felt crushed by the weight of what she hadn't known. So this was what war was like? The China Incident had started in the summer of her eighth birthday. She and her friends used to play on a triangle of vacant land behind Yokohama Station, bounded by the Katabira River, the Tōkaidō Line and the local line. In one corner of the boggy reclamation was a patch of swamp fringed by thick bamboo grass. Hajime had brought back the tallest, "the whopper," and they'd decorated it and made wishes on it for that day's festival of Tanabata: July 7, 1937. Since that day, war had grown familiar to Setsuko. What a lot of letters she'd written to comfort the troops since those early schooldays. She'd calmly told soldiers whose names she didn't even know: "Please fight for the country with all your might."

The soldiers marched away gallantly through streets lined with gay Rising Suns, and the Imperial Army went from victory to victory. Even the homecoming processions for slain heroes as military bands played funeral marches had a solemn beauty. War always appeared before Setsuko decked out in finery. Nowadays, though, she might write to her brother "Take care of yourself," but not "Please fight for the country with all your might." She had learned how hard her young heart must have been to have written that message over and over without a twinge of pain.

There was something alarming in Dr. Ishizuka's face when he came into the room. Naomi, too, had a very strained expression. She looked quite unlike the Naomi who'd gone to welcome him and bring the tea tray. Setsuko had been away from the factory with a cold for over a week and should really have been spending this Sunday resting up in readiness for work the next day. But it had been too long since she'd visited Naomi at home, and Naomi was often unable to get away to visit her, and so she'd finally decided to come—though not without guilty feelings. Now, though, it seemed time for her to leave.

"Naomi, you have a visitor, and I really should be going."

"No, it's all right. I'd like you to stay and listen to what Dr. Ishizuka says, too." Valiantly playing the hostess, Naomi offered tea and found an ashtray for the doctor. "Doctor, this is Setsuko Ōizumi, who I've told you about before. This is Dr. Ishizuka, an old friend of Papa's who is also Mama's doctor. Since both of you are very important to me, I hope you'll speak your minds freely." There was a kind of desperate seriousness in her voice. Setsuko sat down again helplessly. "Doctor, you've found out something about Papa, haven't you?"

Dr. Ishizuka murmured assent as, behind his spectacles, he kept his eyes fixed on a corner of the table. The family had known only that Naomi's father, Professor Hayao Niwa, was in the Tokyo Detention House; since the previous summer he had ceased to communicate with them. He didn't write, and he even refused his wife Tōko's visits for the quite incredible reason that he didn't wish to see her.

"How old are you now, Naomi?" There was a deeply troubled shadow over the doctor's expression.

"Fourteen. Why do you ask?"

"Does that make you still a child? Or are you an adult by now?"

"That's a difficult question." Naomi sighed, then smiled ruefully. "I think I'm sometimes like an adult, sometimes like a child."

"Well, then, listen to me today as an adult. Niwa is—"

"Is Papa . . . ?" Naomi broke in sharply. "Papa is dead, isn't he?"

"No, he's not dead yet."

"Not yet? Then . . ." Naomi jumped to her feet, then lowered herself into the chair again. "Is he very ill?"

"He's in such poor shape it's a wonder he doesn't fall apart, but

52

I'm not sure I'd call it an illness." Dr. Ishizuka spoke heavily, with frequent pauses.

"Please tell me the plain truth, Doctor. I'm standing in for Mama today, so I'll be very grown-up." Naomi glanced at Setsuko seated beside her and reached out a hand to find hers. When Setsuko had taken it in a firm grasp, she repeated: "Please, tell me the truth."

"Niwa càn't see. It seems he began to lose his sight around last June. Naturally he couldn't write any letters. At the same time his teeth started falling out, and they say he's lost the lot by now. Half his hair's gone too, and what's left is as white as an old man's. He refused to eat most of the prison food—he has such expensive tastes. It seems Tōko was taking him food parcels practically every day, but not much was getting through to him, and then on top of that he got into the guards' bad books through his typical arrogance. Apparently your father wanted to keep Tōko, and you, Naomi, from knowing what a wretched state he was in. After they moved him to the hospital he had some trifling quarrel with the doctor in charge, and then he refused further treatment because the doctor said it was wasting good medicine to use it on the likes of him."

Naomi's hand, grasped in her own, began to tremble so violently that Setsuko was startled.

"Naomi, what's the matter?"

"I don't know. I suddenly got the shakes, and I can't seem to stop." The chattering of her teeth made it hard to catch the words. Her bloodless face was paper-white. Dr. Ishizuka found a rug to wrap her in, then asked Setsuko to hold her while he quickly gave a sedative injection. The sight of Naomi in her arms, clenching pale, dry lips and knitting her brow as she held herself in control, made Setsuko realize what a violent shock the doctor's report had given her.

In time, when the trembling subsided and a little color returned to her cheeks, Naomi fell into a deep sleep. Dr. Ishizuka put her to bed and stroked her hair fondly for a moment. "Poor child," he murmured under his breath. He sat at the foot of the bed with sagging shoulders. "Poor child, she's too young to suffer like this. But in a way her mother is more of a child than she is. I never saw the like of it. Father and mother both, they're a pretty pair. A pair of absolute fools." There was nothing Setsuko could say. She too was deeply shocked by the doctor's story. Though she didn't understand what was happening, the agony of despair had pierced her heart. It was like no pain she'd ever known, and it would never leave her now.

"I'm afraid I've got a patient today whom I simply can't leave. I have to get back to the clinic. I'll send a nurse over at once, but could I ask you to remain here in the meantime?" It was impossible to refuse. Setsuko could see the worried looks on her parents' faces as the short winter's day darkened, but it couldn't be helped. The large silent house seemed bleaker than ever. She'd have to prepare Mrs. Niwa's evening meal of invalid's gruel. She closed the curtains and lowered the blackout shade over the lamp, then tiptoed to the kitchen. The big dining room and adjoining kitchen had seen better days: once, she'd been told, gatherings of students would join the family for dinner. Having helped Naomi earlier with lunch, she knew more or less where things were kept. As she washed a handful of rice in a small earthenware pot and put it on the charcoal brazier, Setsuko thought how lonely Naomi must be, working alone in this big kitchen, its emptiness blowing through the room like a wind. Dr. Ishizuka had called her father and mother a pretty pair, a pair of fools. Couldn't they have found some other way, before Naomi was brought to such loneliness? At the same time, however, as she sat on a chair she'd fetched from the dining room and heard the gruel bubbling on the brazier at her feet, Setsuko wondered if it was entirely Naomi's parents' fault.

Dear Setsuko,

Do you remember how, last time we met, I couldn't wait to get to work? When I thought how I'd be doing my bit for Japan, I was more eager than anybody to be mobilized for labor service. I wanted to do the work of three—to do the share of my unpatriotic Papa and Mama as well as my own. And what do you suppose they've had us doing at the factory for the past week?

On the first day we toured the premises, on the second we had a physical examination, and ever since then we've been weeding. And even that we only do for an hour or so each day. Half the time we sing songs or read books in a disused, dilapidated building full of cracks that let in the light and drafts. It's so stupid I can't even bring myself to get angry. No one takes the weeding seriously, but it doesn't matter how slack we are—there are sixty of us, after all. What'll we do when we run out of weeds? What'll happen in winter, when they die?

Mama suggested I leave school. If you're going to pull weeds in other people's yards, she says, then you might as well cook the meals here at home. I can tell she wants a servant around while she drinks shōchū from morning to night. As it is I'm usually the one who does our turn on the neighborhood duty roster, and takes part in air-raid drills, and collects our rations. So I've missed plenty of school already. I used not to care—Mama and I were agreed on that point, at least. But when I knew we were going to a factory, I announced that I wouldn't take any more days off, and Mama couldn't do anything about it. And now look: here I am making an earnest effort to act like a true Japanese, and you'd think they were deliberately thwarting me. Or does it mean that a proper Japanese does as he's told, however stupid his job is? (In other words, in this case, he does nothing.)

Anyway, I'm not enjoying these days at the factory. I sometimes even think seriously about taking Mama's advice and presenting a medical certificate for a fake illness so I can stay at home. What would you do, I wonder? I'd very much like to know.

Naomi Niwa

October –

Dear Setsuko,

Today we received a ration of peanuts. Under-fifteens are counted as children, i.e., it's been confirmed that I'm still a child. Peanuts, one bag, @ 20 sen. I've resolved to save all the rations that aren't perishable. Can you guess why? To pass them over to you. Since you won't accept things from the black market, Mama and I will eat those (after all, we're traitors already!) and I'll give you all the stuff you can't object to. The ration situation isn't too good now, but according to Mama it's going to get much, much worse. She says people like Setsuko who take things too seriously (Mama said it, not me) won't do what they could to save their own lives. It's no joke! I can't let you starve on these rations that you take so much to heart.

So, next time we meet there's a present of peanuts for you. That's a promise. I'm awfully excited to think that it's not black market, and therefore acceptable.

Dear Setsuko,

It was a sparkling clear autumn day today. The headmaster arrived unexpectedly as we were weeding. He said "I've come to set my mind at rest about how the first-year girls are getting on, and I'm relieved to find that you're working very hard, and aren't fussy about what you do." Do you suppose he was being ironic? Then he did some weeding with us, and asked after my grandfather. I didn't

know what to say (because I don't know how he is), so I said
nothing. Then he pulled up some weeds that had turned red and
taught me the word for them, kusamomiji, *or maple grass.*

That was all, and yet tonight I feel somehow relaxed, less on
edge. Simply because of a few kind words. I understood today how
much they can mean. And, too, I'll be seeing you three days from
now. I haven't been sleeping well lately, but tonight I expect I'll
sleep like a baby. Good night.

Naomi Niwa

The Eastern Military Zone was issuing repeated reports of
bombers over Yokohama. Today's were different from the usual
raids. A heavy tension filled the factory atmosphere. Most of the
workers and students lived in the coastal belt between Tokyo and
Yokohama. Though Tokyo had been almost totally devastated since
the first raids at the end of the previous autumn, Yokohama had suffered little damage so far. It was even rumored, plausibly enough,
that Yokohama would escape the bombs because of its historical ties
with America.

Atsuko Yokoyama, who'd been away from her seat for some time,
came racing over and held out a scrap of paper for Setsuko to see. It
was part of a postcard, charred, but not too blackened to make out
the words "Kamitan-machi, Kanagawa Ward, Yokohama City."

"The sky's pitch-black over Yokohama, and bits of ash are blowing
this way." Atsuko had a nervous tic in her cheek. She clearly wasn't
coming back to her bench. "Our house is in Maita-chō, Minami
Ward. But Kanagawa and Minami are a good way apart, aren't they?
Do you think it'll be all right?"

Setsuko was silent. After she'd finished her own work, she was
thinking, she'd have to do Atsuko's share as well.

"You live near Yokohama Station, don't you, Ōizumi-san? They'll go for the station before anything else, won't they?"

A scream sped through Setsuko's mind, and deep in her heart she cried "Mother!"

Living so close to the station, her family had expected the worst when the air raids intensified. They weren't sure whether or not to count themselves lucky that the compulsory evacuation had stopped a few houses short of their own. "We've got no old people or small children to worry about, so let's stick it out in Yokohama," her father had said, and both Setsuko and her mother had agreed unhesitatingly. "If everybody fled the cities, what'd become of our industry? We can't carry on the war with nobody to man the factories, can we? When they've bombed us once, they'll leave us alone." Setsuko had been sure her father was right. What she hadn't foreseen was that the bombers, striking with such extraordinary fury in the middle of the day, would catch her mother at home alone.

Shortly before noon, when the bomb damage in Yokohama was known to be severe, the students who lived in that direction were ordered home urgently. As Setsuko hastily ate lunch and made ready to leave, she heard Jun Sawabe's tread on the stairs. Not caring who saw him, he walked straight up to Setsuko and looked intently at her. "Ōizumi-san, they say the trains aren't running and we're to walk back to Yokohama. You haven't been looking at all well for the last few days. I expect you've got a fever right now, haven't you? I wish I could see you home, but I'm afraid I can't. Try not to get left behind, whatever you do. A friend of mine goes as far as Yawata Bridge, and I've asked him to keep an eye on you. His name's Okamoto. I'm getting behind in my work, I must go. Will you be all right? Okamoto's a good fellow, you needn't be shy—if you have any difficulty, tell him at once."

"Thank you." Only after Sawabe had turned away did Setsuko raise her head. The little contact she'd had with him had always been indirect, through Kiyoshi Harada. Now he'd thought of her and taken action of his own accord. At a time like this! To her consternation Setsuko felt her heart leaning weakly toward him, and she was unable to lift her face while he was looking directly at her. Halfway up the stairs Sawabe paused and twisted around. This time she didn't conceal her face.

The outside door opened and Atsuko Yokoyama cried "Hurry, Ōizumi-san! Section Three is the last to go!"

"Hatono Girls' High, Unit Three," Setsuko called. "Reporting to the square in front of the main building!" As she turned with a quick bow and left, Sawabe leaned heavily against the railing, craning to watch her go till he was almost doubled over.

"The Keihin Road is impassable, so it looks like we'll be making quite a detour. But we should still be home by evening. So let's keep our spirits up and all stick together. You must be absolutely sure to inform the leader before leaving the line if you meet your family or are near your house. Those who can't make it to work tomorrow will be excused, but please be sure to inform your school of any change of address, or if you are evacuating from the city."

The leader of the student unit gave the announcement in strong, ringing tones intended to boost morale. Most of the students were girls who came from the districts south of Kawasaki on the Yokohama side. Several teachers and male students were to escort them. They set off, with the party that had farthest to go—beyond Yokohama Station—marching in front, followed by those for the station, for Koyasu, and for Tsurumi. The girls hardly said a word, so intent were they on walking. They had to get home, whatever the chaos they might find there. They knew that the bomb damage was extensive, but there were no details. They could do nothing but walk, each staring at the classmate's back just ahead, their faces made blank by a torment of anxiety. Beyond the town the quiet fields of early summer lay untouched; farther ahead a leaden sky awaited, and their imaginations made free with the hellish scene they would find below it; but no one put it into words.

"Setsuko Ōizumi of Hatono Girls' High. Where are you?" A boy jogged back from the head of the line, calling at the top of his voice. Startled, Setsuko raised her hand. It must be the student Sawabe had mentioned. "I'm Okamoto of Shōwa University. I understand you're not well."

"No, I'm all right, thank you."

"Are you sure? I'll be up at the front. Call me if you need help." Okamoto—who wore the strap of his cap pulled tight under a tense square jaw—spoke rapidly then dashed back to the head of the column.

Masako Hayashi, at Setsuko's side, wasn't a talkative girl. Strictly speaking, Setsuko belonged in the party heading beyond Yokohama Station, but she'd joined the station group in her eagerness to avoid Atsuko Yokoyama's company, and she was secretly relieved, for had Atsuko been at her side she'd have cross-examined her mercilessly until satisfied about Okamoto.

Though Setsuko had insisted she was all right, she was deeply comforted by Jun Sawabe's having noticed what she was silently enduring. It was true she hadn't been feeling her best for the past few days. Clearly, the problem was her fever. The day trip she'd made to Gunma to see Shōichi Wakui must have overtaxed her strength, especially since she'd not been well to begin with. But she was glad she'd done it. She kept the gray notebook with her at all times, in her duffel bag, to remind her of Naomi. However, the notebooks containing Mrs. Niwa's translation of the last part of *Les Thibault* had sat on her desk, with the book, until she'd gone to see Shōichi Wakui and left them with him. If she hadn't taken them to him for safekeeping, they might have been burned to a cinder in today's raid. "Naomi," she said under her breath, "I did do the best thing, didn't I? I've no right to the notebooks, but Shōichi Wakui was close to your father,

60

and he's the right person to keep them, wouldn't you say?" It was almost two months since Naomi and her mother had died. No one but Shōichi Wakui, in Setsuko's eyes, was capable of fully appreciating the love of humanity that the author had put into the character of Jacques Thibault, nor worthy to live out the human aspirations that filled those two notebooks.

The fever hadn't caused her to miss a single day's work, but as her own health grew worse she worried increasingly about Shōichi Wakui's condition. She remembered the greasy perspiration on his forehead as he walked her to the temple gate toward evening, leaning on a stick and breathing heavily between fits of dry coughing. As if poking fun at himself, he'd said "It's against my principles, you know—to shorten my life by coming to see you off!"

It was a long march. Setsuko had no idea where they were. The one thing that made it bearable was the greenery on either side of the road. Sometimes there were patches of forest, sometimes beds of rice seedlings ready for planting out, sometimes yellow-tinged fields of barley. The houses dotted about this landscape were, of course, unscathed; there was no doubt in anyone's mind that the attack had been concentrated within the city limits. The group for Tsurumi split off first, the girls taking leave of one another without a word, merely raising their hands slightly. There were sure to be friends among them who wouldn't see each other again. Setsuko felt a sudden longing for each of her classmates, even those she'd never had much to do with till now, as she wondered how many would show up at the factory next day.

About the time they passed Kikuna Station on the Yokohama Line, they came upon the first family of air-raid victims they'd seen. An old man in civilian uniform was pulling a two-wheeled cart which was pushed from behind by a woman with a baby on her back. The cart was overloaded with possessions of every sort, and, tucked in among the quilts, a little girl's flushed face caught the eye. It was covered in perspiration, her hair plastered flat to her scalp, but she slept like a log. From a small pair of wooden sandals with a broken cord that were tied to the side of the cart, it was clear that the child had walked most of the way and must be too exhausted to notice the heat.

Masako Hayashi let out a sudden moan and covered her face. "What's wrong, Hayashi-san?" Masako shook her head violently in reply and rubbed her eyes roughly with the backs of her hands. Then, half turning a tearstained face to Setsuko, she said "My mother and little sisters... ," but broke off to steady her voice against rising sobs. The sight of the homeless family had confirmed the girls' worst imaginings. Every one of them saw her own kin in that group.

The closer they came, the more distressing were the scenes of victims fleeing the city center. Fewer were hauling household goods now: they had obviously only had time to stuff a few personal belongings into a bag on their way out. When an infant was carried past, limp, with his head tied up in an amateurish triangular bandage that came down over his eyes, Masako burst into tears again.

"How old are your sisters?"

"Five and two. My little brothers were evacuated to Tochigi in a school party. My father is away on business in Hainan. My mother has a weak heart and she's spent half the time in bed since my baby sister was born." Masako spoke brokenly through her sobs, no longer caring how she sounded. "Will they be all right, Ōizumi-san? They will, won't they? They'll hold on till I get home." Till she got home: even if the family had escaped safely, how was she planning to look after her frail mother and little sisters? This slip of a girl, doing poorly in school, whom Setsuko had never thought of as anything but quiet and shy, stunned her with the fierceness of her love for her family.

Near Ōguchi the unit leader made them assemble in an open space for a fifteen-minute rest. Before they'd realized it, strange-smelling sooty air was pressing in on them. The area that had been hit lay just ahead. Setsuko felt chills creeping up her spine: the green of the grass she sat on was flickering behind her closed eyelids as a flamelike blue. She heard Jun Sawabe's voice again: "Try not to get left behind, whatever you do."

"I'm all right, thank you." Answering the voice in her heart, Setsuko felt Sawabe's firm support.

"Very soon we'll be inside the bombed area." The leader stood up to address the party. "We'll probably have to make our way through places where there've been fires, so everybody watch your step. Hold your neighbor's hand, and don't lag behind the girl in front. When you leave the column, be sure to tell the nearest person. Does everyone understand? Right, let's put our best foot forward!" From the coldness of Masako's hand, Setsuko could tell her own fever must have worsened.

Not far from Ōguchi they said goodbye to the girls from Koyasu, and soon afterward entered the built-up area. Unfamiliar smells of burning hung waiting for them in a vast smoke layer. Inside there was a strange, turbid time zone, neither day nor night. Gusts of wind stirred up red flames here and there among collapsed houses. "Is so-and-so here?" The man who went by shouting for so-and-so of such-and-such an address must have just reached home, fearing for his family's safety. Suddenly there were shrieks from the girls in front, and the column wavered. "Someone's dead! With white hair! It's an old lady!" Those further back detoured in a half-circle across the road, putting its width between themselves and the old woman's body. They averted their faces, though some took a frightened peek. But in another quarter of an hour not one of them was shrieking or turning away from the sight of the dead. It was all they could do to avoid stepping on the bodies strewn about the road like so many charred pieces of wood. Ahead, what had been city streets that morning were gone, leaving only a dimly lit, leaden waste.

"Ōizumi-san, this is where I turn off." With a hard squeeze of her hand, Masako bowed and dropped out of line.

"Good luck," Setsuko called, but she sensed the futility of her words. The house was sure to have burned, and if the surface of the road was littered with the blackened bodies of strong men, how could her mother and sisters possibly have come through the inferno alive? What could Masako hope to do? Without her companion's hand to hold, Setsuko was overwhelmed by fatigue. Weak-kneed, she stumbled over a small stone and fell. Okamoto, whom she hadn't noticed at the back of the line, came running to assist.

"We've just passed Higashi Kanagawa, so we're nearly there."

"Yes. I'm all right. I can walk by myself." A girl in glasses, someone she didn't know, fell into step with her. When it occurred to her to look back she saw only four or five people behind them, with Okamoto bringing up the rear.

Crying "Mother!" the girl in front darted from the line and hurled herself at one of the figures by the road who were gazing urgently in their direction. "Mother! Mother! Mother!" she cried, while the figure simply held her tight and nodded. When the line had passed, though, she bowed her head deeply toward the rows of backs. As others in the lead split off, the girls behind Setsuko moved up to fill the gaps until she found herself last in the line. And when Okamoto stretched out a solid arm for her to lean on, she no longer had the strength to refuse.

"Keep going! Yokohama Station is up ahead." What *was* up ahead? What lay in wait for Setsuko after the hours of desperate walking? Would her mother have come through safe? A sound drifted back from the head of the line, a long "Oh!" that could have been a gasp of amazement or of sorrow. The line came to a standstill

64

on Aoki Bridge. The high railway bridge, midway between Higashi Kanagawa and Yokohama stations, spanned the many local and long-distance lines running into the central terminal. But was this the city of Yokohama that lay beneath their eyes? Low hills were unexpectedly close at hand; they appeared foreshortened and continuous from Goshoyama to Nogeyama, as if they'd cleared Takashima-chō, Hiranuma-chō and Tobe in one stride. At the thought of the houses and lives that had crowded between those hills, Setsuko was dumbfounded: so many separate existences wiped out in barely half a day. As she stood rigid on the bridge, leaning on Okamoto's arm, tears at last flooded her cheeks.

Another spring's grass shoots were pushing up on the embankment where the two girls were lazing. A train for Sakuragi-chō crossed overhead, then the sunny noontime tranquillity returned for a few moments. A platform announcement was heard from Yokohama Station, the loudspeaker booming, so they couldn't make out the words. Each time a train passed on the elevated Tōyoko Line the swamp surface below quivered, rippling the shadows of the bridge girders into elongating and contracting zigzags.

"When I was little," Naomi said, "students were always coming to our house and discussing difficult subjects in Papa's study. I loved to listen, and I'd sneak under Papa's desk and keep very still. Afterward I'd surprise Papa by repeating something I'd half heard—like 'Those denominations, you know.' He'd say 'So you were in your hidey-hole again, were you?' and he'd grab me and squeeze the breath out of me."

"My grandmother who died," Setsuko said, "was a very hard worker. Some factory used to dump coal cinders on that empty lot over there, and she'd be there waiting to pick them over. It was my job to collect the coke she dug out and carry it home in a little bucket. To keep from getting sooty she wore a towel over her hair, an apron, and cotton work gloves. Yes, now I remember, she made me wear all those things, too."

"Papa and Mama," Naomi said, "have always quarreled a lot. They'll be listening to a record, and if Papa says 'Ah, yes, Kreisler is unquestionably the world's finest violinist,' Mama will say 'Nonsense! Huberman is by far the best!' Then there's a dingdong argument until they suddenly tell me to go to my room because they're going to make up. They must have a special secret way of making up."

"Just before I started school," Setsuko said, "my brother and I used to catch minnows in that ditch over there. He told me they're what people use to make dried whitebait, which is a favorite of mine, and I said I wanted some. So he arranged our catch on a flat stone in the sun, and after a bit he said 'They're done. Try them.' I told Mother about it when we got home, and caused a real fuss. I was given an antidote and put straight to bed, and my brother got a dreadful scolding and no supper."

The two girls, seventeen and fifteen at their next birthdays, were bereft of a future, and though their real lives had yet to begin they were talking like old folk lost in reminiscences. Or perhaps this *was* their old age, for the hour of their death was near, as they well knew.

Setsuko decided to stay where she was till daybreak. Though the yard was small, it was still incomparably better than the murky confines of the shelter. The garden soil had been turned over until it more or less resembled a ploughed field; it was no mattress, but it wasn't as hard as she'd expected. She shifted her head a little to dislodge a stone, then stretched her arms and legs. They were so heavy she wondered if they could already be half-dead. She kept both eyes wide open and stared straight ahead. There was nothing that stood between herself and the countless stars sprinkling the sky an infinity away. Darkness hid the scorched earth and the rubble, and all the ugliness around her had vanished. The wind was fresh and faintly salty. The Katabira River, barely thirty feet off, was brackish close to its mouth in the angle of Tokyo Bay. Setsuko's grandmother, who'd died some years previously, used to call the river "the sea." "Don't play by the sea," she'd say, "it's dangerous." Ignoring her, Setsuko and her friends would sit and chat on the bank, dangling their wooden sandals by their big toes. Factories had been built along the riverside and the dark waters were no good for swimming as in their grandmothers' day, but Setsuko remembered the time a great school of jellyfish came upstream, the teeming translucent discs, large and small, transforming the familiar waters till they really could have been the sea.

On the afternoon of the second day after the big air raid, a corpse was found in the Katabira. The body was swollen to twice its normal size and the face and neck were green. Only the protruding eyes and the lips, turned back like torn edges, were a bright pink. Several men from the neighborhood association who happened to be nearby dragged it up to the road and identified it by a clothing tag: the man was a worker at a nearby iron foundry. His surviving workmates soon arrived with a cartload of wood to burn the body on the spot. This was directly below the railway carriage that sheltered a number of the homeless, and Setsuko among them. The flames and the sunset glowed together in its broken panes, and Setsuko learned what a long time it takes to burn a human body on a bonfire.

Her face grew chilly and damp with dew. Autumn was in the air. Wanting badly to hug something, Setsuko raised her heavy arms to clasp her own shoulders. Their cold stiffness brought back an earlier sensation to the palms of her hands.

"There might be a yard on the other side of this wall, and it might be an exercise break, and Papa might be leaning on his side of the wall just like I'm leaning here, mightn't he? If I close my eyes and think about it, gradually the wall doesn't seem so cold—it gets as warm as Papa's back. In the end the wall disappears, and I can feel his back with mine, although I can't see him."

Naomi was standing, not moving a muscle, hard up against the tall, thick concrete wall that ran the length of the Tokyo Detention House. The long lashes of her closed eyes trembled faintly and, though her cheeks were dry, Setsuko was afraid she was going to cry. Without a word she put her arms around Naomi's shoulders and hugged her tight. The shoulders were hard and cold as stone: body warmth could not take the chill out of a concrete wall, any more than her thoughts could reach her father in solitary confinement deep inside.

"You're with your dear father now, aren't you, Naomi?" Speaking the words eased her heart, and her arms slipped from her shoulders. "It's all over. I wish it was over for me too." As the sky in the distance grew hazy and the farthest stars began to pale, Setsuko made her way back to the shelter, repeating her movements in reverse. But not before she'd fixed in her mind the image of the last starlight she would see in this life.

November –

Dear Naomi,

The air assault on the mainland has begun at last. We knew all along it was coming, and now it's here.

Though actually it's not my first air raid. One Saturday afternoon in April, just after I entered Hatono, a friend and I had left school a little later than the others because we'd been on cleaning duty, and we were strolling down the hill when an air-raid warden yelled at us "You can't walk there! Get out of sight!" We heard bang! bang! and saw puffs of smoke in the sky. We hid behind a tree and said to each other "They're taking the drill very seriously today, aren't they?" What a shock we got later when we heard that an American plane had dropped real bombs that day! The banging we heard was our side's antiaircraft guns.

That was kid stuff compared to what's coming, though. Quite a while ago, I heard some scary talk about how the whole of Japan would be bombed and everyone would die. It came from Hajime's friend's brother, the one I've told you about. I refused to listen at the time, but now I'm not so sure. I know now that I must do my part and fight with a new resolve.

The other day the people just down the street from us were evacuated. Lots of friends I've known since we were very young will be going away to the country, and I'll miss them. But it's all for the nation, and they'll still be living the life of Japanese in war-time wherever they are, so we told each other to keep up the good work.

Naomi, I said this when we met, but I'll say it again: I don't think your factory was ready to receive students. I'm sure you'll soon be able to work as hard as you want. Don't be disappointed— do your best. For me.

Bye for now.

Setsuko Ōizumi

Her father still hadn't come home by nightfall. By then mother and daughter had set up temporary residence in one corner of a damaged railway car on a siding of the Keihin Express, and had retrieved three cans of supplies they'd buried in the garden.

"You got back safely, Setchan, and so will your Dad." Setsuko's mother, Miné, maintained a deliberate calm. Their plan to use the three large, square, lidded cans—of a type used by wholesale confectioners—had worked very well. They'd dug a hole just big enough in the yard, and in an emergency they were to stuff their belongings in the cans, put them in the hole, and cover it with an iron sheet and as much earth as they had time to spread over the top. Being alone when the time came, Miné had instead piled their three sleeping pallets over the iron sheet and thrown a couple of buckets of water over them. In spite of her haste, perhaps because there was nothing flammable near the hole, the middle and bottom pads had come through just a little charred around the edges, and the cans were safe and sound under the iron.

"When your Dad gets home tonight, let's celebrate." They would feast on canned boiled mackerel and vegetables in soy sauce. As Setsuko watched her mother, unperturbed, take out their chopsticks and bowls from one of the cans and with the aid of a cloth transform a train seat into a neatly laid table, she savored the joy of having found her safe.

"Your Dad was late leaving for work today because he had a headache. He'd barely left the house when the sirens started. If only he'd been even later I wouldn't have had to cope on my own. Still, I wasn't hurt, so I can't complain."

"I guess not . . ."

"Dad won't know where to find us. We don't want him getting lost. Shall we go and stand on Banri Bridge?"

"Well . . . ," Setsuko mumbled. The night air would soon chill her to the bone, she knew, as her temperature showed no sign of going down. She was thankful that the darkness deceived her mother's sharp eyes. "I'm a bit tired. I think I'll stay and keep an eye on our things."

"Yes, of course, you must be worn out after the walk from Kawasaki. At least *you* got back by nightfall, even if your father didn't. If neither of you had come back, I don't know what I'd have done."

Miné laid the two good sleeping pallets one on top of the other on the floor, and, saying "You get some sleep. I'll wake you when Dad gets back," she jumped down from the car, grunting with the effort. Setsuko crawled between the two pallets and stretched out, limp with exhaustion. When she pulled the top pad up to her chest a strong smell of burned cotton hit her. And when she closed her eyes the tumultuous hours of the afternoon came back vividly. What had Masako Hayashi done? Had the little red-faced girl asleep on the handcart reached a resting place for the night?

Picking her way among corpses in the smoke-filled streets, Setsuko could only comprehend the extremity of what was happening in immediately personal terms. But when she stood on Aoki Bridge and surveyed the devastation on all sides, the word "air raid" had taken on meaning for her. With it had come an association from the past which was now causing her deep anguish. In elementary school, Setsuko used to write letters of encouragement to the brave pilots of the long-range bombing squadrons. *"I saw a newsreel at the movies. It was about a bomber with the Rising Sun painted on the side dropping bombs on the town of Shanghai. From where the bombs hit, a big cloud of black smoke went up. Someone said banzai. I shouted banzai too."*

Now Setsuko began to wonder how many Chinese those bombs had killed, how many families' houses and lives they had taken. China was an enemy nation, the Chinese were enemies of the Japanese. It had therefore been a matter of course to drop bombs without compunction, to wipe out their existence. It followed naturally that America was now bombing Japan, killing Japanese and destroying their existence. If American children saw the rubble of Yokohama in their newspapers and shouted the English equivalent of "banzai," it was only to be expected. But was it really? Setsuko was anguished by the growing feeling that it didn't make sense. Naomi's words in the gray notebook—her last message, as it had turned out—came to mind. *"I wish from the bottom of my heart that I'd been born in an age without war. Why do we make war, when we're all the same human beings?"* The crushing weight that burdened Setsuko's chest was not due only to her fever.

She must have dozed off, because the next thing she knew Miné was rummaging through the cans at the foot of her bed. "Mother, when did you get back? What about Father?"

"We can't expect him tonight. It's raining, and pitch-dark, too. Nobody can move till it gets light." Miné found the emergency ration biscuits and reached out, groping for Setsuko's hand to give her a share. "Aren't you running a temperature, dear?" she asked, startled. "Your hand's so hot!"

"I'm all right. It's nothing." Setsuko managed to hide her agitation and sit up briskly in spite of an aching head. "I got hot walking, and then I went off to sleep under a mattress, so no wonder my hands are hot!"

"Well, I hope it's nothing more. We'd really be stuck if you got sick at a time like this."

"I'm thirsty. Is there any water around here?" Setsuko tried to get up, but sank dizzily to her knees. She caught her breath, afraid Miné would see, but it must have looked as though she'd tripped.

"Watch your step. It's too dark to be moving around. Yes, there is some water—I'll get it."

Setsuko took the flask and drank and drank. She could feel the cool water going all the way down to her stomach. "Ah, that's good."

"Have all you want. There's more where that came from." Miné sounded pleased with herself.

"The tap still works?"

"It certainly does. I made sure it would. We had such a bad time

72

without water after the earthquake of '23. I used to have to go over to Kanagawa and carry it back in buckets on a pole. I'd never done that before in my life, you see, and I let so much slop over on the way that I got home with the buckets half-empty. I could have cried. So today, when the time came, I turned the tap on hard and left it running. There's a kink in the pipe but the tap's working fine. We won't go short of water."

"That was good thinking, Mother. Thanks."

"All in a day's work. When you and your Dad are away, it's my responsibility, isn't it?" After they'd made a meal of ration biscuits and water, Miné lay down at Setsuko's side. "All we need now is for Dad to show up safely."

"He'll be all right. A man can look after himself."

They closed their eyes, but neither slept. After a while Miné whispered, "That was a terrible thing today, wasn't it?"

"Where did you shelter?"

"Where? All over the place. First I got into our air-raid shelter, but I had a feeling the house would be hit. So I ran and put the cans in the hole. Later I stepped out for a look, carrying only Grandma's mortuary tablet, and there was smoke everywhere. It was kind of lonely by myself, so I joined a crowd of the neighbors in the shelter out front, the one the neighborhood association dug. But something didn't seem right, so we took a look out and the fires were closing in on all sides. The master of the Wakamatsu Inn told us to get out or we'd roast. He said to make for an open space with nothing around it that would burn, and then we split up. I got under Banri Bridge, climbed onto a sort of stone ledge about a foot high, and held on tight to a girder. Fire bombs kept spiking into the river right before my eyes and sputtering out. Well, I thought, America's not stingy with its bombs. I could hear a frightened child whimpering in the other corner and the mother saying 'hush, hush,' and patting its back. Turned out to be the people from the barbershop. Their three little ones were all safe—wasn't it lucky? Well, that's enough talk. Let's get some sleep. Tomorrow's a big day."

But Miné herself didn't stay quiet for long. "Do you know the first thing we have to do in the morning, Setchan?"

"Well, it's hard to know where to start."

"We start by making a latrine."

"A latrine! How?"

"Leave everything to me. Remember I'm a veteran of the great earthquake, and I know just what to do. Well, then, let's go to sleep. This time I mean it. Good night."

"Good night." Setsuko was acutely aware of the anxiety behind her mother's excessive cheeriness: she must be sick with worry over Father's failure to return. To spare her mother more pain, Setsuko resolved never to let her find out about her illness.

By first light Miné had already dug a fairly deep hole in a corner of their yard. She chose two of the least damaged timbers from the house and laid them across the top, parallel and spaced apart. She then made four more holes around the first and drove charred beams upright into the ground. "Now we just give it roofing iron for walls and it's done. How're you getting on?" As instructed, Setsuko rinsed the soot off four sheets of iron under the tap. To her relief, her fever seemed much better this morning. It was heavy work for the women to prop three sheets in place and lash them tight, leaving a single opening. The fourth sheet they leaned across the doorway to screen it from view. "The trick is to cover the hole with earth before it gets too full, and start over in another place. I'll let you have first go, Setchan." Miné smiled proudly. Then she dropped her voice: "Setchan, what about your monthly?"

"It ended just a while ago."

"That was lucky, wasn't it? Mine is due soon. Though I expect I'll be closing down in that department before much longer. A woman has problems at a time like this, doesn't she?" Mother and daughter gave each other a look of resignation and laughed. With the daylight, people began to pass by their yard from wherever they'd spent the night, going toward Yokohama Station. Miné brought out a brazier she'd stored in the shelter, lit it, then hunted up an iron cooking pot from the kitchen debris.

"Let's have that special meal today," she said, but the gruel she made with precious white rice got cold and Setsuko's father still hadn't returned.

"I'll ask down by the station," Miné said, no longer attempting to be cheery.

She came back a short time later, her face pale. "They say it's very bad along the Keihin Express Line, and around Hinode-chō and Kogane-chō there are great piles of bodies. Even if your Dad's train had come at once, I don't think he'd have had time to reach Sugita. I'm going to search for him, dear. Put some water in the flask for me, will you?"

"I'll go with you."

"You wait here, Setchan. It wouldn't do to miss him on the road. I'll be back by evening." Miné hastily made ready, put some of the cold gruel in Setsuko's lunch box, took the water flask, and was gone. Her mother's desperation unnerved Setsuko all the more. Many of the corpses she'd seen around Kanagawa the previous day had been men, she could tell. The fact that he was a man, and traveling light at the time, didn't guarantee his safety. Left alone, Setsuko found her knees trembling and realized she was quite unsteady on her feet. There was a lot to be done—the house site had to be cleared and the rest of their emergency gear unearthed—but all she managed was to take a piece of pale wood from the bottom of the bathtub (which, being full of water, had survived the fire), and write on it with a charred stick: "The Ōizumis are in the train at the back." She propped the sign up conspicuously then took the leftover gruel and returned to the train.

75

But she walked right into calamity: the three small children from the Sugawaras' barbershop were rifling Miné's hard-won cans and stuffing themselves with the emergency ration biscuits. Though not close by, their mother was there in the carriage, hunched against a seat as if she had dozed off, with her back firmly turned. When they saw Setsuko the children's mouths turned down and they burst into tears all at once, before she got out a word. Their mother came scurrying at the noise, but all she said was "Don't be hard on them, they're only little, and I promise we'll make it up out of our next rations."

From farther down the aisle, the woman who lived next door to Setsuko muttered loud enough to be heard: "I told her over and over that the children were eating the Ōizumis' biscuits. She went on pretending not to know. What a nerve!"

"Would you please take the boys over there? I want to have a rest." Setsuko avoided looking at the mother's face while she gathered up scattered towels, Miné's comb and mirror, and their other things. But even when she'd burrowed between the two pallets the children's insistent wails of "We want some more" still reached her. Pressing her hands over her ears she barely managed to escape her neighbor's pointed muttering.

"The parents are irresponsible, if you ask me. Not saving food for emergencies, when they've got three small children—it's a disgrace!"

Mr. Sugawara, the barber, was a disabled veteran. He'd lost his leg below the knee in the China Incident, and he complained of having to stand all day as he worked, his artificial leg tapping the floor and his face darkened by fatigue. Was it so irresponsible for such a family, with three small children and little chance of supplementing their rations, to be caught without emergency supplies? Even in Setsuko's family of three grown-ups, it had taken self-control to save the food.

A hatred with nowhere to go whirled in Setsuko's breast. She hated them all violently: the three infants who'd stolen the hard biscuits, and the mother who'd turned a blind eye; the woman from next door with her loud remarks; and herself, carefully shutting up the last few pieces while the children cried for more.

Toward noon, Okamoto came to see her. "Are you feeling any better?" he asked.

"Yes. Thanks for your help yesterday."

He had bicycled over. "My house wasn't touched. But the bomb damage is far worse than I realized yesterday. I'm glad your mother was safe." Setsuko didn't mention her father. He might still come home. She had a sort of superstitious fear that if she said anything he really wouldn't return. Okamoto unloaded a bulky cloth bundle from his carrier and held it out.

"My mother and sister insisted." He seemed embarrassed at pressing the gift on her. "They said even when people save a mattress they tend to forget the pillow. I believe there's a pillow and some personal things in here. I got a scolding when I tried to take a look—those are not for a man's eyes, they said. Please don't be offended if there's something odd in there." His earnestness reminded her of Jun Sawabe. And his mother's and sister's kindness was the more touching for being so unexpected. "I'm going to the factory now," he continued. "I have to satisfy Sawabe that I've delivered you safely home, you see." He went on his way laughing, while Setsuko watched with tears in her eyes.

A man crossed the site at that moment and approached a group that was tackling the job of cleaning up. "Do you want any rice balls?" he asked in a low voice. He opened the wrapper he carried to display rows of white rice balls the size of a child's fist set out on a tray. A crowd formed around him, but Setsuko remembered the leftover gruel and went back inside the train. Having to worry about theft among all these familiar faces was unsettling, and she was relieved that this time no one had interfered with the three cans during her absence.

"Here, wait a minute, you!" The voice of the woman next door rang sharply across the rubble. "You've got to be joking! What d'you take us for? Ten yen for one of these piddling little things! That's really kicking people when they're down! Call yourself a Japanese, do you? Go for the cops, somebody, I'll turn the creep in!" Setsuko stood up in time to see the man take to his heels with his bundle. The Sugawara children came in, fretting "We want rice balls," and kept it up for hours afterward.

That evening, rations of one rice ball per person were distributed. An official of the town association bellowed an announcement to the waiting line: "These were made especially for the bomb victims by the women's association over Hiratsuka way."

"Yummy, yummy!" At the children's excitement, even the woman from next door said huskily, "There's something about this that brings a lump to the throat," (though in fact it had more soybeans in it than rice).

Miné came back after dark. When she learned that Setsuko hadn't seen her father either, she sank down on the spot and said quietly "I'm afraid it may be hopeless." The blackened bodies she'd stepped over in the ruins of Kanagawa were still on Setsuko's mind when, just two days later, she reported for work as calmly as if nothing had happened.

November –

Dear Setsuko,

Today I finally handed in notice of temporary absence from school. Starting tomorrow, I'm not going to the factory. I don't care what anyone else says, but I do want you to know the true reason, Setsuko.

The factory holds an annual variety show for its employees on the company's anniversary. Some professional entertainers are brought in, and the staff do amateur turns. This year it was decided to do the parting scene between the Lord of Kusu and his son at Sakurai, with a woman worker playing Kusunoki Masashige and one of the students as Masatsura. Don't ask me why, but the official of the Welfare Section who was organizing the show tried to give me the part of Masatsura. Then the teachers sent for me and said it should go to Yoshiko Akiyama. They were quite right: if I'd gone on as the son of a warrior revered for his loyalty to the imperial dynasty, both those noblemen would have rolled in their graves.

I'd been intending to turn it down anyway because it's not my kind of role, so I didn't mind that, but the incident resulted in the whole factory finding out about Papa. And it started all over again, just like when I came to Hatono High this spring. As you know, I've been very well behaved recently. No lateness or days off, and I still think I worked the hardest at the weeding, though I grumbled to myself. I haven't been the least bit rebellious, even when treated unfairly. But I'm worn out. I'm sick and tired of persevering among a lot of people who will never accept me. When all's said and done, I'm a traitor's child. Never again will I forget my place in life and aspire to be a true daughter of the nation.

You must be pretty disgusted with me for making such an important decision without consulting you. But I couldn't stand it any more. Please don't be cross.

There's another thing: Mama is ill. I thought about giving that as my main reason so you'd let me off lightly, but I didn't want to lie to you, Setsuko. Mama's illness was sort of an extra. She'd been saying that her stomach hurt, but she blamed it on Papa and wasn't in any hurry to see the doctor. "All my troubles have given me an ulcer," she said, "and going to a doctor won't help." Then about a week ago she brought up blood. Dr. Ishizuka, an old friend of Papa's, said it really was an ulcer and she'd better go into the hospital, but Mama wouldn't listen. She insists she's not moving from Papa's study till he comes home. Since she won't listen to reason, we've turned the study into a sickroom by moving the sofa and table out to the bedroom and bringing in Mama's bed. If I'd requested leave because of Mama's illness, I'd have had to go through the whole traitor business again, so I had the doctor write me a medical certificate (it says I've got "amyloid infiltration of the lungs") and handed it in today with my notice of temporary absence.

So from today I'm a nurse-housekeeper. Now that it's turned out to be a genuine illness, Mama's become awfully quiet. She just sleeps and never talks, so I've got time on my hands. For one thing, she's told me not to worry about cleaning the rooms we don't use, or else I'd never get through. (We're only using the study, kitchen and hallway.) Most of the families around us have evacuated, with someone staying behind to mind the house, so there isn't much work to be done for the neighborhood association either. I may be in for a boring life—no factory, and not much to do for Mama. So I searched for a novel that'd take forever to read and came up with Eiji Yoshikawa's Miyamoto Musashi. *It's so long I've kept a respectful distance up till now.*

Setsuko, I've become a genuine traitor at last, but you do understand it wasn't by choice, don't you? I haven't much to show for my efforts, but I really did try.

Naomi Niwa

The morning sun had filtered unnoticed into the shelter. The indirect light, almost too soft for early autumn, bathed Setsuko's upper body where she lay. All the beams and struts that she thought she'd seen with her fingertips in the darkness now loomed in the half-light. At the back of the shelter the ceiling boards were already beginning to rot, and her mother had often said "We must fix that up before the typhoon season." Wasn't it about that time of year now? Her mother had been afraid a storm would bring the ceiling down and flood the shelter. But it didn't bother Setsuko this morning. She hadn't felt so good in ages. Her fever had gone, she was fully conscious, and—she could scarcely believe it—the violent cough and phlegm had eased. Pleasantly languid, she felt the radiance on her cheeks after several sunless days and basked in its smell. She slowly raised her right hand to shield her eyes. The knuckles of her thin fingers were strangely swollen and there were wedges of black dirt under the long nails. Perhaps it was mud; or it could have been her own grime. A frown gave way to a tight sad smile when she realized that she was covered from head to foot in the same filth. When her mother died, Setsuko had heated pots of water and tenderly washed the body, but no one would be left to do the same for her. She groped in her duffel bag for a mirror but then hadn't the courage to examine her face, and after a moment's hesitation she put it away. At the border between dream and reality her fevered mind had drifted a number of times to thoughts of what would happen after her death, but they were too painful to focus on consciously and in daylight. I'm going to die, but there's no one to stay beside me. After my death I won't be buried. With the war over, I wonder how many bodies are lying out in the open with no one to dig their graves? "Go to the sea, There lie the drowned, Go to the mountains, There lie the grassy corpses. Let me die at the side of my glorious prince, And I will never look back." She'd sung that song with its solemn, stirring melody since her childhood, but only now did she understand what it had been saying.

"Boys and girls! On the proud occasion of the inauguration of this Student Corps here today, let me express my earnest hope that you will discharge your duty as noble warriors of industry, serving the country and His Imperial Majesty with all your might." The company president had thrust out his chest and bellowed this speech. That was at the end of May; two and a half months later, his tone was tragic. "Boys and girls! On the occasion of the disbanding of this Student Corps here today, I join you in offering His Imperial Majesty our humblest apologies for a dishonor unprecedented in history, an unconditional surrender, due to the inadequacy of our efforts."

The earth had swayed and Setsuko had remained on her feet with difficulty, a greasy sweat breaking out on her forehead as she gasped for breath. Despite her high fever and extreme weakness, violent indignation raged in her breast. Driven by uncontrollable passion she made her unsteady legs carry her to stand firmly in front of the president.

"I have nothing to apologize to His Imperial Highness for. I have done nothing to regret. Why have they surrendered? Weren't we supposed to fight to the last on our home ground? Weren't we going to give our hundred million lives in a fight without surrender?" The assembly was stunned. The president turned away, white-faced, then brusquely shoved Setsuko aside with a hand on her chest.

"What are you saying, girl?"

Her determination spent, she collapsed and was carried to the infirmary. Setsuko regained consciousness to find her homeroom teacher, an elderly woman, sitting despondently by her bed, not bothering to wipe away the tears that wet her cheeks.

"Are you awake, Ōizumi-san?" Stopping Setsuko as she tried to sit up, the old woman looked at her red-eyed. "Ōizumi-san, it's just as you say. You and the others have nothing to apologize for. We ought to be apologizing to you. I've been thinking about this ever since I heard the Imperial Rescript yesterday. About what I've done, what I've taught my pupils. Please forgive me, Ōizumi-san."

Setsuko remembered how this elderly woman had read Atsuo Ōki's poem to her second-year literature class, her voice as high-pitched as a tense little girl's:

Do not say farewell, my friend,
Nor talk of everyday things,
Nor of life and death.
What will there be to say
At the farthermost ends of the sea?
Strike the great breast of one who offers his ardent blood,
Hold the full moon in your wine cup,
Drink and take strength for a while.
I am bound for Batavia,
You to conquer Bandung.
Though we part this evening,
Together let us see
The shining Southern Cross again some night.
Do not say farewell, my friend.
See how the clouds pass,
The clouds pass silently,
Where sky and water meet.

"I should have insisted that you rest and recuperate." The old teacher's remorse was unremitting. "Although I knew you were ill, I was moved by your dedication. What good was I as a teacher!" Firmly declining her offer to accompany her home and apologize to her parents, Setsuko parted from the teacher at Yokohama Station.

That violence of emotion was gone now from Setsuko's breast. The rage and sadness had sunk quietly into its depths. Atsuo Ōki had written: "Though I leave my country's shores And cross the seven seas To the farthest outpost of the south, In death I shall be near His Majesty, In death I shall be near His Majesty." But the verse from the *Manyōshū*, "Go to the sea," was more fitting both for the bleached skeletons on southern beaches and for Setsuko whose bones would soon bleach in a bomb shelter near Yokohama Station.

On the way home from a day's work, Setsuko would be unbearably tired. Afraid to face her weariness squarely, she would use any spare moment to open a book and escape to a make-believe world. On the crowded trains she would be wedged in so tightly in the middle of a car that her feet would even lift off the floor. As long as the train wasn't delayed she actually enjoyed this, for it meant she didn't have to support her own weight. Both hands were full, anyway, keeping hold of the duffel bag and the air-raid hood which hung crossed over her shoulders, in case they were torn loose in the crush. A friend might be beside her, but they'd have nothing to talk about, and as the other girl's stop approached she would have to think quickly to reach the exit. It was all right at larger stations like Yokohama, since more people got off than on, but at the others the incoming rush of people would force the girl right back to the middle of the car if she was too slow.

Setsuko had been borrowing books from Jun Sawabe one at a time, but with no electric light after the house burned down her reading made little progress. Only on Sundays could she sprawl on the riverside embankment if it was fine, or against the steps of the shelter if it rained, and lose herself all day in a book. Thus the time she spent waiting for her train was precious. Normally it wasn't long, but the train was quite often late, giving her an unexpected chance to read. As the train drew near, however, she'd have to snap the book shut and put it in her bag; if she was too engrossed to notice the train, it would be jerked from her hand and lost forever in the jostling crowd.

Setsuko was unaware of her mother's death until she came through the ticket gate at Yokohama Station. Even when she recognized the head of the neighborhood association and the woman from next door leaning forward over the wicket, she never thought for a moment that they might be waiting for her. But when the woman suddenly covered her face and cried "Setsuko-chan, I'm so sorry!" she guessed that something had happened to her mother. "I'm so sorry! There was nothing anybody could have done. It was all over in a second." The woman tried incoherently to explain until they were all seated on the stone steps of the post office beside the station. Then the association head—a taciturn man at the best of times—broke his silence at last to tell Setsuko that her mother was dead. The deliveries of special rations that had begun immediately after the air raid were at an end, and supplies reaching those who'd stayed in the area had dwindled to a trickle since the previous channels of distribution had been wiped out. Nor could these people turn to the black market, for they had no stock of possessions to barter. They were all starving. Then they'd heard perhaps the first good news since the raid: rations of new potatoes were on the way as a rice substitute—a good ten days' worth. Amid a mood of expectancy, the woman next door and Setsuko's mother (who were rostered for duty that day) had set off with a handcart for the temporary distribution center at a local girls' school; but when the cart returned to a waiting crowd several hours later, it contained Miné Ōizumi's body.

"Nobody took shelter even when the sirens went. No one expected a second attack on a bombed-out area like this. Two P-51s came in from the sea, heading toward Hodogaya. Then, grinning all over their faces, they zeroed in on the ration line and killed Mrs. Ōizumi and the others. With machine guns going rat-tat-tat-tat.

They flew very, very low—people said they could see their round heads in the cockpits."

It was barely a month since Setsuko had lost her father, and now the one person she had left was dead. Still listening to the man's explanation, Setsuko heaved herself to her feet and began slowly walking. Part of her mind was numb, uncomprehending. At the same time, against her will, she already understood everything. She walked more and more slowly, caught between a desire to run and a refusal to move another step. So many people close to her had died that death itself was almost a commonplace; in that sense, though it was her mother this time, there was nothing special about her death.

People were clustered in front of the neighbors' house. "It didn't seem right to put her in the shelter, so she's at our place." The woman had dried her eyes on her apron and returned at last to her normal self. Her two sons had built a hut on the site on their days off from conscripted factory work, so that the family had at least a roof over their heads.

"It could've been me. If the bullet had been a foot to one side, it would've been me." Miné had been laid out on a coarse blanket over bare floorboards; a square of new bleached cotton over her face was a vivid white. Setsuko lifted a corner of the cloth: her mother was frowning slightly, but her expression gave no other sign of pain. Setsuko replaced the cloth and shut her eyes in silence as tears ran down her cheeks.

"Let's hold the vigil here, Setsuko dear." There was a small bell and candle beside the headrest, and the bell chimed at intervals as a neighbor offered a prayer. They'd asked all around the neighborhood, said the association head, but no one had any incense.

"You've been very kind. Thank you for all you've done, but I'd like to take my mother to the shelter. I want to be with her . . ." The onlookers could find nothing to say as Setsuko broke off and hung

86

her head. Soon afterward the neighbors' sons carried the body to the shelter, and their mother escorted Setsuko.

"Sit with your mother, Setsuko dear, till you feel you've done all you can." As the job of collecting rations for the neighborhood association was rotated among its members, everyone gathered at the house had the same thought in mind: "What if I'd been on duty today?" The neighbor left to go home, but reappeared to whisper: "I've heard they won't take bodies for immediate cremation, even at Kuboyama, unless you can provide the wood. If you've any cigarettes or saké we can arrange it."

"There's some new silk cloth . . ." Remembering the bolt her mother had once brought out with a secretive smile, Setsuko found it in the tea chest at the back of the shelter and handed it over. "Will this do?"

"I'm sure it will. Such a nice piece of material—what a waste. You could have worn it, dear."

After seeing the woman out, Setsuko closed and barred the shelter door. As she kept watch in the dim light of a flickering candle, her pent-up grief overflowed. "Mother! Mother!" She clung to the cold, stiff body, wailing and beating it with her fists. Her mother's death had come as the ultimate breach of faith. Her father and brother might never return, but her mother, who'd survived that massive air raid, had seemed bound to share her fate until the very end. Though she gripped Miné's hand till her own was chilled to the bone, it would never regain its warmth. The cold of despair gradually penetrated her heart. There was nothing she could do. She must endure this hard reality and make a new start, even if despair lay at the end of the road. After weeping alone for a time, Setsuko went outside. The night sky was heavily overcast and the damp air felt muggy on her cheeks. Wood from the house, which her mother had carefully broken into kindling and tied in small bundles, was stacked near the shelter entrance. As she filled the cooking pot with water and lit the brazier, Setsuko's tears returned. How in the world could she go on alone tomorrow? In her weakened condition she had relied totally on her mother's day-to-day care.

She poured hot water into a washbasin and, carrying it to the shelter, gently washed her mother's face, then her hands. Next she undid her mother's jacket, and her eyes were drawn to a single spot. A small, deep hole gaped below the left breast. The bullet had pierced the heart from the back. There was not much of a stain, even on her undergarment. The hole in her back was smaller still.

Japanese lining up for meager rations on a bomb site were still enemies to American eyes. A mother who'd lost her husband, seen her son off to the front, and made her home in a dugout shelter while worrying silently over a daughter who concealed her illness rather than leave the production line: she, too, was an enemy. Her father had said they wouldn't bomb the same area twice; but as long as there were Japanese alive in the ruins it would remain a war zone. Setsuko had made one more painful discovery: so that's the way it is when there's a war on.

Late at night the woman came over again from next door. Even though there'd been a death, someone still had to deliver the rations, and her two sons had collected them after dark and gone from house to house. "You should offer some to the departed and have some yourself," said the woman as she held out a bowl of boiled potatoes. Then she went to Miné's side, almost crawling in the tight space, and joined her hands in prayer. "Ōizumi-san, I'll look after Setsuko like my own daughter. You can set your mind at rest on her account, at least." She struck the bell, joined her hands in prayer, then paused to wipe her eyes and blow her nose; when she faced Setsuko her voice was steadier. "We've got the wood. I've asked them to bring it tomorrow morning. I'll get my oldest boy to take the day off and go to Kuboyama. After all, it was nearly his own mother he had to take. He can't argue with that. Bear up, Setsuko dear." As Setsuko stepped outside to see the woman home, she found a fine spring rain soundlessly veiling earth and sky.

December –

Dear Naomi,

Today was Imperial Rescript Day, and during the parade I was surprised—though it's nothing new—to see how the boys' ranks have thinned. So many have volunteered and gone to the front.

I don't think I've told you this yet, but at the factory I'm considered a bookworm. (Isn't it a laugh? They got that idea because I spend the lunch break reading the books you lent me.) One of the boy students lent me a book he recommended. His name is Harada, and he's tall and handsome, so there's a lot of talk. It's just one misunderstanding after another, and all very embarrassing.

The books you lent me are over my head as it is, but Harada-san has come up with one called Jean-Cristophe. *He's a great admirer of the author, a Frenchman by the name of Romain Rolland. Then, several days ago, Harada-san signed up for the navy. He'll be exactly a year behind my brother. Before his departure he introduced me to his friend Jun Sawabe. He's put all his books in Sawabe-san's keeping, and he wants me to borrow them freely even though he's not here. He said it would make him very happy to know that although he can't read his precious books himself, they're being enjoyed by someone else. So I'm getting carried away and racing through lots of novels. Whyever did I hate them so? What a mistake that was, and how lucky for me that we became friends! Please lend me* Les Thibault *again soon. I think that now I might be able to understand some bits a little better. I especially want to go carefully over the parts in your mother's notebooks,*

L'été 1914 *and the epilogue. I decided on this while thinking over your reason for being absent from school.*

To be honest with you, I think it's a great pity that you're missing school. I would've liked you to try even harder, and I can't help wishing I could stand by you and give you encouragement. If it was me, I don't think I'd leave the ranks for any reason while the war is on. I'm sorry to be so hard on you. But I don't want to lie to you, either. Please don't think I don't understand your point of view—of course I do. It's just that I wouldn't ever leave the factory, no matter how tough the going got.

But we'll always be friends, whatever happens. Don't think I'm angry. I'm only sorry, and vexed with the people around you who drove you to it. I think you'll feel better and return to the ranks when your mother recovers from her illness. I pray that day will come very soon.

Setsuko Ōizumi

People walked abruptly out of one another's lives. A friend who'd waved goodbye on a Kawasaki Station platform died the same night in a fire-bomb attack; a kindly factory hand who'd given the girls a share when the workers had a special ration of frozen mandarins received his draft papers and wasn't at his bench one morning. As each day began, the exchange of greetings was full of the joy of having met again, while eyes meeting in farewell each evening held the sorrow of knowing that this might be the last time.

Ayako Matsui, the young teacher who'd supervised Setsuko's class since April, said goodbye to the girls quite suddenly one day. She was a graduate of Nara Women's Teachers' College, and her home was also in Nara. "Are you evacuating, Miss Matsui?" The girls were dissatisfied to think that their homeroom teacher, who'd been like an elder sister to them, should be going home. They felt she was abandoning them.

"Well, um . . . ," Ayako Matsui stuttered in a way that wasn't at all like her usual animated self.

This made the girls still more emotional. "Miss Matsui, why don't you see it through with the rest of us?"

"I wanted to, but . . ."

"Why don't you, Miss Matsui? Why not?"

Miss Matsui lowered her head at the sharpness of their questioning.

"Miss Matsui isn't just going to evacuate!" Atsuko Yokoyama, always in the know, spoke up with adult malice. "Miss Matsui is going home to marry her fiancé!"

Gasps of "What!" escaped the girls' lips, but the murmurs soon died away to an awkward silence.

"I'm sorry. I wanted to see it through as a member of Hatono Girls' High, but under the circumstances . . ."

The girls remained silent, acknowledging that if that was the reason then Miss Matsui would not lightly be persuaded to stay. Yet when they thought of all the male students and factory hands they knew who were leaving one after another for the war, it seemed absolutely immoral to marry one's fiancé. Instead of the wave of regret that should have washed over the parting, there was a cold hardening of their feelings; neither Ayako Matsui nor the class knew how to bring the scene to an end. At that moment one of the girls burst out tearfully: "This is awful! This is going too far!" It was Yōko Ōno, who worked in the office; she rushed forward and stood protectively between teacher and pupils as she cried "Miss Matsui isn't getting married for her own sake! Her fiancé is a wounded veteran, he's lost his eyesight. Miss Matsui has to take care of him and his parents."

"No, you're wrong." Ayako Matsui lifted her pale, tense face as if she'd finally gathered the resolve to speak. Her voice was low but clear. "It's true my fiancé is blind and his parents are getting on in years. But I'm not getting married because he's a disabled veteran, or for the good of the country. I'm getting married because I want to. It's for my own happiness."

The girls missed a deeper truth in the young teacher's words, but they did understand that she spoke with an intensity beyond their grasp, and that whatever it meant it seemed to be very important, not only to Ayako Matsui, but to themselves. Someone sobbed "I'm sorry, Miss Matsui," and set all the girls sobbing at once. The brief half hour allowed for the farewell was gone before they knew it. The girls returned to their places, their eyes red, and went back to work with a will, hardly talking, bewildered by the passions that had found their way into their breasts.

Ayako Matsui's replacement was a surprise: Okimura, the man who'd been duty teacher on the day that Naomi got into trouble. He had more gray hairs, and with his pinched features looked more morose than ever. But in the lunch break he came up to Setsuko, who was reading alone, and said lightly "It's been a while, hasn't it? Where's that plucky first-year girl these days? Is she still as high-spirited as ever?"

"Poor Naomi, a lot of things have happened to her."

"Hasn't her father come home yet?"

"Her father died. Her mother is ill. I believe she's given notice of temporary absence from school."

"Has she? Yes, I suppose she would." The world was a harsh place also for Okimura, who'd formerly been an English teacher specializing in literature. When he said "I suppose she would," he spoke with deep fellow-feeling as if he himself could hardly keep going. Okimura, too, was to disappear from their lives little more than a month later; drafted—the last thing he'd expected.

"I'm forty-six this year. I'm graded B2. What sort of soldier do they think they can make out of me?" He'd stood by Setsuko's bench and ground out the words, jabbing the palm of his hand with the tweezers. He never showed his face again. It was the custom to give those leaving for the front a send-off with a song and three rousing banzais, but Okimura refused this. He dispensed also with a teacher's farewell to his pupils; instead he simply disappeared.

When they saw his successor, the elderly woman teacher of Japanese, Atsuko snickered: "This one should stay. It doesn't look like she'll be getting married, or going to fight either!"

In the gentle light Setsuko slept. She hadn't slept so soundly for a long time. The elusive scenes that came and went in her sleep brought a smile to her lips, just as they'd brought a touch of brightness to what little youth she'd had.

She seemed to be in a classroom. Her classmates had exercise books open on their desks. The teacher stood at the blackboard, chalk in hand before a geometry problem. It was a complicated figure. The teacher was busily explaining something, but she couldn't hear a word. Now he was asking a question. No one raised her hand. The teacher approached Setsuko, still speaking. His right foot dragged: it was Sawabe. Their open books were not on their desks but on their workbenches—oh, it wasn't school, it was the lesson that the male students gave the schoolgirls before work each morning. While learning math and physics in those classes, Setsuko had nurtured her growing affection for Sawabe.

She seemed to be in a library: bookshelves lined the walls. The corners of the room were in impenetrable darkness, but the place where everyone had gathered was light and airy. They were reading at desks, side by side: Naomi, Jun Sawabe, Kiyoshi Harada, even Hajime and Shūzō Wakui, all absorbed in their books. Setsuko gazed fondly at each. Harada rose and, after asking her to read his books, vanished through the dark shelves. A Rising Sun flag bearing his classmates' signatures was draped over his shoulder, just like the ones Hajime had worn, and the echo of his marching boots rang after him. Sawabe raised his head and said quietly, "We should study hard while we have the chance." He held a new exercise book and pencil. "I expect this is what you need right now, Ōizumi-san." It was just after Setsuko's house had burned down.

Setsuko was standing in the debris of a fire. Where she'd seen bookcases there were thick wadded layers of ash. One by one, flakes rose into the sky, where the print stood out faintly in the sunlight like shadowgraphs. There'd been a huge volume of paper ash in Professor Niwa's gutted study. In tears, Setsuko sifted the heaps with both hands. Naomi and her mother must be there. But however deep she dug there were still more burned books. And no sign of Naomi. Setsuko tumbled forward into the hole she'd dug. She struggled desperately as ashes smothered her face.

Then she woke and was really smothering. After a struggle to clear her throat of phlegm, she finally took a sip from the water flask and settled down. She could still feel the wet ash plastered on her fingertips.

She had stayed away from the Niwas' house for a long time. After Naomi's father died, Setsuko was troubled—tormented, rather—by a sudden realization that her friendship toward Naomi had been false. Her health had been too poor for the trip to Naomi's house, it was true, but the main reason for her hesitation was shame: she was ashamed to present herself before Naomi. And while she was hesitating, Naomi had come to say goodbye.

"I think I wanted you to accept me no matter what I did. Thank you for being so kind for so long. Now, please work for the good of the nation and don't worry about me." These parting words, written in the gray notebook, had moved Setsuko so much that after waiting impatiently for her next day off she'd gone to Naomi's address. But the quiet leafy suburb had been reduced to scorched earth. The fire

needed no explanation—there had been air raids almost every day—yet for a moment Setsuko felt a stab of bitter remorse.

"Mama says if she had her wish she'd die holding Papa's urn, buried under his books as they go up in flames. We don't even have an air-raid shelter, you know." Naomi had said this offhandedly when she had visited Setsuko the previous Sunday. Her quiet, adult manner gave her a lonely air. There was nothing Setsuko could say, faced by the depth of love shared by Naomi's family—an extraordinary love, perhaps.

The word "ruin" was exactly right for that square space marked out by concrete walls. There could be no doubt now that Mrs. Niwa, with the professor's urn in her arms, had lost her life there together with her daughter Naomi. When she placed her hand on the bronze gate embossed with vines, it scraped open with surprisingly little resistance, just a slight sound like a shriek. One step inside, a yellow flash that could have been dizziness passed before Setsuko's eyes; but it was a memory of the dense beds of daffodils that had bordered the path to the front door. The rows of massed gold had been dazzling in the midst of a wintry landscape. Setsuko's last visit had been at the end of February: her first since Naomi had learned of Professor Niwa's death. The Naomi who had thrown herself sobbing convulsively against her breast with a cry of "Setsuko!" was gone now. Before she died Naomi had despaired even of their friendship. The thought left Setsuko stunned by the enormity of her own betrayal. What on earth had she been doing to Naomi this past year? Had she made friends with her only to betray her in the end? Worse still, she couldn't ask Naomi's spirit to forgive her; she didn't think she had any right to be forgiven. On the last page of the gray notebook Naomi had written "*I still love you, Setsuko*," and Setsuko's love for Naomi, too, was unchanged. She could not yet understand that the cause of the rift between them went beyond their own wills. She stood still in the burned house, and a deep sense of futility blew through the hollow place left inside her. The despair of betrayal had been a greater shock to Setsuko herself than to Naomi. As she closed the gate she noticed a wooden tag with the message "Please forward all communications to the following address: — Kamisuwa, Suwa City, Nagano Prefecture," but she went away without hesitation. Naomi's short life of fourteen years had ended, and Setsuko was nearing the end of her sixteen. She had convinced herself that she had caused the rupture of their friendship; but a family like Naomi's could never have survived such an age. The age itself was nearing an end—it was a matter of months away—though no one could have believed it then.

From outside the shelter came children's voices. The shrill squeals brought the excitement of their unseen game into the opaque quiet of Setsuko's world and made her smile. "No war can go on forever. And human beings are the toughest creatures on earth, you know. There's no sense being in a hurry to die. *You must live*, whatever happens." Shōichi Wakui had squeezed her hand and told her this with an almost violent urgency, though his grasp was weak and his voice halting. Were those the Sugawaras' children she could hear? The barber had had the presence of mind to rescue his kit when he fled through the flames of his burning shop, and now he was doing a brisk trade, seating his customers on a cushion atop piled stones from the foundations. To house his family he'd put up a lean-to against the railway embankment, barely enough to keep out the weather, but at least the children were no longer starving. Even in defeat the locally garrisoned soldiers all had some supplies of food, and while waiting to board trains for their hometowns from Yokohama Station they'd sit on the stone seat of the Sugawara Barbershop and have a good shave, leaving the children something to eat as payment.

Setsuko no longer felt the rage that had overwhelmed her at the disbanding ceremony. If they had fought on home ground, one hundred million Japanese sworn to die before they would surrender, those children would have had to die too. Those young lives and spirits would have been extinguished in terror and pain and they wouldn't even have understood why. They have a right to go on living, and the strength to do it, Setsuko thought. For their sakes, if no one else's, I should rejoice that the war ended before an invasion reached the home front. Shōichi Wakui's words came back clearly: "Even when a war is lost, people's lives still go on." And Naomi's, in the gray notebook: *"Every war comes to an end, and when peace is restored Paris rises like a phoenix."* But what about those who'd already died? It was agony to think of those who would not rise: the dead would be left where they fell at the ends of the earth while the living would come home with their knapsacks of clothing and food. Whether they had gone to the front or stayed at home, the people had staked their lives for country and Emperor, and after they had lost, the country and the Emperor were still there. Then what had it all meant? Adrift and floundering in despair, Setsuko slipped back into a restless sleep. By afternoon the fever had returned; her brief respite was over.

"Setsuko dear, isn't there any place you could evacuate to in the country?" Early on the morning of August 16, Setsuko was woken by the loud voice of the woman next door.

"Evacuate? But the air raids are over."

"I'm not talking about air raids. Japan has lost the war, so you young girls had better hide out in the mountains, *or else.*"

"Or else what?"

"Well . . . come outside for a bit."

Setsuko was groggy. The loss of Jun Sawabe in the August 13 raid on Kawasaki Station and the walk home to Tsurumi had drained her strength and left her laid up all the next day, racked by fevered nightmares. Though less feverish on the morning of the fifteenth she still wasn't well enough to walk and had to stay home from work. She was present, however, when the neighborhood association assembled in the Kiyōken Restaurant to hear the important radio broadcast at noon. Back in the shelter her fever worsened, but she was determined to report to the factory the following day. The imperial broadcast—an unfamiliar voice through static—had left the listeners uncertain of what they'd heard, some insisting it had been a rescript urging preparedness as the battle reached the mainland at last; but Setsuko knew intuitively that it had been an announcement of surrender. Was it possible? Jun Sawabe and Shōichi Wakui had been absolutely right. What had everyone at the factory done? They had been supposed to take their own lives at the moment of defeat. Had her classmates died the previous day? She had to get up or she'd never make it to the factory. Though groggy, she didn't seem as feverish now.

She crawled out of the shelter to a startling sight. People were waiting in amazing numbers—how had the ruins of Yokohama concealed so many? The line came from the direction of Yokohama Station, crossed Banri Bridge, and stretched almost to the Tōyoko Line overpass.

"These folk are after tickets to get the women out of town and into hiding. Why don't you go down and have a listen to what they say? 'Imperial Army,' my eye! They know what's coming, because they did such wicked things when they were in China. With soldiers like that, you can see why we lost the war!"

Once again Setsuko only dimly guessed the truth, but she wanted to block her ears and shut out its ugliness. She heard two men talking as they urinated by the river. "Between you and me, I heard of a corporal who screwed a thousand Chinese in the free-for-all when we took Nanking. You're another, aren't you?"

"Not me. It was more like ten."

"And now you're heading for the hills and getting your old woman out of harm's way, eh?"

"Why not? She's not much to look at, but I'm not going to let 'em hack the old woman about, am I?"

Though not loud, the voices traveled clearly on the wind and left a dark stain of dishonor on Setsuko's tender innocence. While she had walked in a lantern-lit procession in honor of the fall of Nanking, one dot in a beautiful winding cordon of light, had such vile acts been going on in that city? Was this part of what went on in wartime, too? As if to shove aside the horror that had filled Setsuko's body, her neighbor gave her a smack on the rear: "This is no time to dawdle, Setsuko dear. Men are all the same at a time like this, whether they're Japanese or American. And it's our side that'll catch it now, remember. I'm going to stay with relatives out Kozukue way for a while, till it blows over. It won't last long, you'll see. Only while they're worked up. When things settle down I'll be back, and we'll pick up from there, eh?"

Returning to the shelter, Setsuko finished the leftovers from the previous day's lunch, eating the rice gruel straight from the pot with a spoon. There wasn't enough to dish up properly and anyway it would have been far too much trouble. When fresh, the gruel could be sipped, but once cold it was as lumpy and congealed as starch paste. Setsuko would have starved long ago if her neighbor hadn't brought her a daily share of their precious food supply, true to her promise to dead Miné that she'd look after her like one of the family. She had no appetite, nor the strength of mind or body to go out and barter for food on her days off. She'd stopped taking a lunch box to work some time ago. The factory canteen provided special rations— a bowl of watery broth with floating scraps of seaweed and greens and a grain or two of the cheapest rice—but sometimes even this was more than she wanted. Her stomach was almost always empty, yet she had no appetite.

Setsuko didn't want to leave the inside of the shelter too messy. She tried to lift the mattress but couldn't budge it, so she straightened it a little and left it at that. She changed her underwear and went outside to wash her soiled things and the dishes. She might never come back, and when she was gone someone would see the place sooner or later. Her eyes took in the crowds scrambling to flee the city before its coming collapse, yet she couldn't stop wanting to believe in something more. The Japan she'd loved, the Japanese people she'd trusted, couldn't be so ugly. But that beautiful something to believe in was not to be found. Not in the turmoil of Yokohama Station, nor in the emptiness of the silent factory: there was no consolation, no answer to her prayer. The divine wind that should have saved the nation from peril had failed to blow; they had not died by their own hands, refusing the disgrace of defeat; all the things she had believed had disappeared without trace and only the elderly teacher's tears, with her plea for forgiveness, had poured into the hollow of her heart. That night, Setsuko's long, grim wait for death began. Hardly touching the bag of parched rice that was her neighbor's last kindness, drinking only water, she would lie in the half-underground shelter as if buried alive.

December –

Dear Setsuko,

I'm very sorry I couldn't come and see you today. When I think of you expecting me all day long, I hardly know how to apologize. I tried writing a postcard but it wasn't enough, and besides it was much too dull, so I got out the notebook again.

I think it's Mama's own fault that she isn't getting better. She follows the prescribed diet for ten or fifteen days, then suddenly gives in and starts drinking again. But the way she looks today, I can't even get annoyed. The worry about Papa has made her so depressed you'd hardly know her. After all, we haven't heard any news for six whole months now. We've asked Dr. Ishizuka to try and find out how he is. I have a feeling he may not be alive. But neither Mama nor I ever say so. If I said such an awful thing out loud, Papa might really die.

Living like this—cooking and cleaning and washing day after day—I sometimes feel very old. Nothing changes. We have a stock of food, we don't take shelter when the sirens go, and these days I don't talk much with Mama, so it feels as if life has been this way for years and will go on like this forever. And yet I might die in an air raid tonight. Isn't human nature funny? I don't mind preparing the meals, but I hate the cold, tiring job of washing. I have an awful struggle to wring the sheets and Mama's cotton kimonos, then to get them dry. If I hang them out in the front yard in the sun, I have to take them in every time the sirens sound. (The people next door make such a fuss if I don't!) So I put them in the backyard instead, where everything's very slow to dry because of all the shrubbery. Though it's silly, come to think of it—the point of taking the washing in is so it won't provide a target for the enemy planes, and just because the neighbors can't see it doesn't make it all right. But I'm more afraid of the neighbors' complaints than of enemy planes. Having to drag that heavy load in and out is worse than being bombed, as far as I'm concerned. You wrote that I'd feel different and get my courage back when Mama gets better, but I don't think so. I think I've degenerated completely. Anyone would (though not you, Setsuko) if they lived alone with Mama.

Lately, even when she's awake Mama seems in a kind of daze. Yet she still makes a beeline for the saké. Since Dr. Ishizuka says I mustn't let her drink, I'm at my wits' end. The first time she brought up blood, Mama herself threw out all the drink in the house. And yet less than a month later she went and exchanged the gramophone and all our records for three bottles of good saké.

She's too friendly with our black marketeer, that's the trouble. He casts his eye over everything in the house and says "I've got someone who wants a sewing machine—will you take ten quarts of rice for it?" Mama gives in every time. She says when the bomb hits it'll all be the same to her. At this rate every room except Papa's study will be stripped bare. But I don't care either. Here we are, worrying whether Papa's alive or dead, when it could be us this very night.

Between preparing meals I read. I've tackled more historical novels since I finished Miyamoto Musashi. *They're what's known as "popular fiction." I was surprised to find authors like Kaizan Nakazato and Sanjūgo Naoki in a corner of the bookcase where I've never noticed them before. I dip into a book, and if it's dull I go straight on to the next. I never used to do that—even if I was bored I'd plod on to the end. But, look, if I'm going to die at any moment, there's no sense being in the middle of a boring book, is there? I'm reading something now called* Kinan Taihei Ki *by an author called Iwasaburō Okino. It's a traditional biography of Tokugawa Yoshimune, written in a very peculiar style. But that makes it more interesting. When I said "I wonder if I should recommend it to Setsuko?" Mama said "I don't think it would appeal to someone who's reading* Jean-Cristophe." *Tell me if you'd like to, though—there are five volumes, and it's quite a good read, for a popular novel.*

I've been wanting for ages to invite you at the New Year, to cook lots of party dishes, and play cards and the Hundred Poets game—you and me and Mama. It would have been fun. But I'm afraid it's no good because of Mama's illness. I don't expect to be alive next New Year, so I guess we've missed out.

If Mama's condition doesn't improve, I may be unable to visit your house next time, too. I wonder if you'd mind coming here instead? I'm sorry if this seems like a summons, but otherwise I'm

afraid I may only see you once a month. No one comes to the
house except the neighbors bringing circulars, Dr. Ishizuka, and
the black-market dealer. I'm alone with Mama, who sleeps quietly
most of the day since she's started taking a new kind of medicine,
so I'm really all on my own. I hope you'll take pity on me and let
me have my selfish way.

Naomi Niwa

One Sunday afternoon in mid-May, Setsuko visited the Wakuis'
house in the Ōmori hills. It had been a simple task to look up
Shūzō's name in Hajime's address book, take the train to Ōmori Station, ask at the police box, and find her way to their grand residence.
But the gate was locked, and there was no answer when she rang the
bell and called. The leafy residential suburb, unscathed as yet by air
raids, was strangely quiet. Setsuko was reminded of Naomi's house
before it burned: though there was nothing obviously wrong, she
had sensed that deep inside it was crumbling quietly away. The
bushes were straggling and shapeless (though people certainly had
more important things to do than keep their shrubs trimmed) and
weeds stood tall.

Since Naomi's death, Setsuko had been worried about keeping Mrs. Niwa's notebooks containing *Les Thibault*. The published
book, which Naomi had wanted her to have as a memento of their
friendship, was not a problem; but Setsuko didn't feel entitled to the
notebooks. True, she could now fully understand Jacques Thibault's
last despairing act; in fact she had even come close to approving it;
but she couldn't accept it for herself. Setsuko had long since passed
a limit that denied her such flexibility. There was no turning back
now, no changing course. The only way to live now was to walk on
down the path she'd taken so trustingly, even if it led only to death,

to the honorable deaths of the hundred million. After thinking hard about who was the right person to have the notebooks, she'd decided on Shūzō Wakui's brother. Shōichi Wakui was, above all, a former student of Professor Niwa. And from what she'd heard he seemed the one person qualified for what she wanted him to do. She'd made up her mind to visit the home of her brother's friend; if there was no one there she would give up. Retreating a step or two, Setsuko stopped to cough, spitting the phlegm into a square of paper. Then for a moment she caught her breath: the phlegm was stained red. It was the first time she'd coughed blood. Setsuko had known she was ill. The factory doctor had told her to return to school and seek treatment, but she'd gone on working and hidden the truth even from her mother. After the initial shock, Setsuko told herself that she shouldn't be surprised to see the bloody sputum when she had only herself to blame.

"What's the matter? Are you unwell?" She hadn't noticed their approach, but there beside her were an elderly woman and a younger companion, probably a maid. Raising her eyes, Setsuko saw a distinct resemblance to Shūzō Wakui in the older woman's features.

"We must have been destined to meet," said Mrs. Wakui feelingly when she'd invited Setsuko into the parlor. "I had to come back to the city to attend to some business. It's my first trip since we evacuated, and I'm only here for three days. I had a visitor yesterday—that's why this room's tidy. Otherwise there'd have been nowhere for you to sit down."

When Mrs. Wakui had studied Setsuko's face, she said "You're very like your brother about the forehead and eyes," then gently pressed her fingertips to the corners of her own. The reminder of Hajime must have brought back Shūzō's image, too, thought Setsuko. "Ōizumi-san was such a fine young man. It's a wonder he could stand Shūzō's company and his selfish ways. We had three sons, but the middle one died young, and the oldest is an undutiful boy, and in the end Shūzō was the only one who stayed with us. So, if you'll excuse my saying so, I used to think of Ōizumi-san as my own son. Daughters don't stay—however many one has, once they marry that's the last one sees of them, you know. But in times like these it's all the same whether one has sons or daughters. They're all scattered, and I rarely get to see even my husband. I spend my time working in the fields with the girl there." She glanced toward the maid, who was leaving the room after bringing them cups of fragrant tea. "I brought a little supply with me for yesterday's visitor. Do go ahead. These days, even plain tea has become a treat, hasn't it?"

Mrs. Wakui's conversation ranged endlessly over her far-flung family of six and returned several times to the son who had died, yet never once touched on the name that Setsuko was waiting to hear. Had Shōichi grown so estranged from his mother? As she kept up her end of the conversation and joined in Mrs. Wakui's laughter, Setsuko was perplexed. She'd imagined it would be easy to leave the notebooks with his family to be passed on the next time they saw him. Her look of puzzlement gradually brought Mrs. Wakui back from the world of her reminiscences. "Gracious, here I am going on about old times when I haven't even asked why you've come all this way to see us. Have you heard something from your brother concerning Shūzō?" When it was Shōichi's name that Setsuko mentioned instead, her face stiffened with surprise and suspicion. "Why, how do you know him?" As Setsuko carefully explained the unlikely connection between Shōichi Wakui and Naomi, in which she herself played a part, she saw Mrs. Wakui's wariness slowly give way to sorrow, and realized that Shōichi had not been at all distant from his mother's thoughts.

"Such an undutiful boy," she said again. "Because of his health, I do try to see that he never wants for anything, but his father has virtually disowned him, and he does tend to keep us at arm's length, you know . . . So Shūzō visited Shōichi before volunteering, did he?

They *are* brothers, then, after all." Mrs. Wakui's eyes dwelled on Setsuko, but her fond gaze was clearly seeing farther. "Those were happy times. When the children were little, they'd all gather round the piano—the three boys and four girls, some on chairs, some on the floor—and listen to me play." Here was another sad mother whose later years the war had filled with misfortune. Setsuko's own mother, and Naomi's, were the same. Setsuko was reminded that no mother escaped misfortune in war.

"Here's my authorization for the tickets back to Shinshū, but the date and destination haven't been filled in yet, so it can be used at any time. We can easily get another. Do take it and pay Shōichi a visit. I understand it's very difficult to get transport from the station, so when you reach Maebashi go to our factory there first, and I'll have them arrange something for you."

The piece of paper that Mrs. Wakui handed her was stamped in red: "Official Business." Setsuko felt a pang of conscience at the thought of the long lines that formed early each morning at the ticket windows, but if she were going to visit Shōichi Wakui there was nothing she could do but accept. And she could see no other way to place Mrs. Niwa's notebooks in good hands.

As she said goodbye to Mrs. Wakui, Setsuko was aware that she probably wouldn't meet the elderly lady again. After setting off into a mild, breezy May evening, Setsuko spoke aloud the familiar precept of perfect hospitality: "We meet but once." That was literally true of everything that happened now.

Dear Naomi,

Hasn't it got cold? I sympathize with you, cooking and washing with your little hands in icy water. How is your mother now? I worry about her, she seemed so careworn and downhearted last time I visited you. I've been away from work for a week now myself, with a cold. I had a high fever for three days, and a bad chest cough, and it's left me quite weak. I suppose I must have been overdoing it, because once I went to bed I was suddenly very, very tired, and I still can't get up even now that the fever has gone. I'll have to stay home a few more days to keep my mother happy. In that time I plan to read as many books as I can.

Now I know how your mother feels when she won't get up for the air-raid alerts. It's such an effort to move. While I had a fever I caused problems by refusing to leave my bed, and my father had to carry me, quilt and all, out to the shelter. But I seem to have timed this cold just right so I can still visit you on our agreed day. I'm not missing that, even if I am missing work—so much for this fine upstanding daughter of the military nation!

If I'm better by then, I'll give you a hand with the cleaning again. Your house is just too big for you to manage by yourself. My mother says she can hardly believe that little girl is coping all by herself. She said it was a pity we don't live nearer, so she could help out every day—and she means it. I really wish I could, too. But with all my good intentions I can't do a thing to help. I'm so sorry.

Even just sitting up to write this has made me so tired my head is swimming. It's a sign of mental slackness to get into this condition with a mere cold. I'm ashamed of myself, when I ought to be making a speedy recovery and working as hard as I can.

Well, let's have a good talk next time I see you.

Setsuko Ōizumi

As fast as she spat out blood, more welled up from her chest. Setsuko was adrift on the red, shifting sea, her paper-thin body drained bloodless. Where am I going? Am I dead already? Then I'll soon be seeing my father and mother and brother and Naomi. It wasn't easy to stay afloat. At the slightest movement she felt herself sinking into infinite depths. Waves of blood were about to close over her. "Ōizumi-san, it'll soon be over." Wasn't that Shōichi Wakui's voice? Yes, he was ill too. Was he drifting on this sea, too, coughing blood? "Ōizumi-san, the war is ending." That voice was Jun Sawabe's. The blood that gushed from the back of his neck had flowed into this same sea. Suddenly Setsuko went under. "Ōizumi-san! Ōizumi-san!" Jun Sawabe and Shōichi Wakui were calling in turn as she floundered helplessly. The next thing she knew she was no longer floating in a sea of blood but standing among charred ruins that stretched as far as the eye could see. Where were all the people who'd been there earlier that day? Aah! She jumped back with a scream: she'd been standing on a corpse. But she landed on another. The expanse of ruins became an expanse of bodies. These turned slowly to bleached bones, and her own were among them. "I'm glad you came," said a skull. Their faces were all alike, but the voice was Shōichi Wakui's. "As I'd been told you were an acquaintance of Professor Niwa, I was expecting a man—and an elderly man at that. I never thought you'd be a young lady." Setsuko woke. In the world that was closed to her in that instant, she left not a skull but the sparkling, deep, dark eyes of Shōichi Wakui.

His sickroom was a long, narrow room—six *tatami* mats in a single row—in the northeastern corner of the main building of Jōshōji temple. "I believe it was originally for the use of itinerant priests. It has its own washroom outside, so one can stay here and not come in contact with the rest of the world." A bed was made up just inside *shōji* screens that opened off the corridor, forming the entry from the main hall, and apart from a radio beside the pillow the room contained only piles of books that littered the floor.

"The chief priest says to use the main hall as it's not needed today." A woman in work pants, her hair tied back so tightly that it almost lifted her scalp, gave the message as she brought two cushions from the priests' quarters and plumped them down in a corner of the larger room.

"Thank him for me, will you?" When the woman had left, Wakui brought his large feather pillow into the main hall, saying "You'll have to excuse me for not getting up." When he was settled with the cushion at his back and the pillow wrapped around his shoulders, his tall body in threadbare shirt and trousers seemed as brittle as a blighted tree. "I was told you have something you want me to keep for you."

Setsuko could never be sure, afterward, why she'd suddenly burst into tears. It wasn't in her nature to cry for no reason, as a spoiled or moody young girl might do. Why had she done such a thing in front of him, and when they'd only just met? The embarrassment still made her hot inside. It was quite dark in the shelter. Above her head she heard someone at the water tap. The thought of people going routinely about their lives was comforting. Wakui had said clearly, "People will go on living after the war's over." Setsuko had refused to think of a time after the war, but his words had been hard to forget. Her mouth twisted in pain. The strange woman had returned with tea and, looking from tearful Setsuko to her disconcerted host, she'd spat out scornfully: "I never thought I'd see the day when the good-for-nothing consumptive would break a young girl's heart! I'll tell the chief priest on you!" Wakui gave a helpless laugh, and though Setsuko hastily called the woman back to assure her again and again that it wasn't his fault, the glint of suspicion was slow to fade from her eyes.

Setsuko bent her head just enough to drink from the flask. Water trickled from her lips, over her neck and down her side, sending chills throughout her body. She must have a high fever again.

After watching the woman go out, Wakui had said, "She's not very bright, you know. She was born in the village and has family there, but people say that some bad men tried to take advantage of her when she was young, and in desperation she begged the chief priest to shelter her. And she's been living here for nearly twenty years now. She works hard—I don't think the temple could get along without her. It was she who nursed the last chief priest for thirteen years—he was bedridden with palsy—and now she's looking after me. The chief priest tells her 'Kiyo, my dear, you're assured of a place in paradise in every reincarnation because you do so much for others.' And she's happy to work even harder."

Behind his nonchalant manner there was a deep concern for Setsuko. He kept talking, patiently and gently, letting her calm down.

"There's a kind of extraterritorial law in force here, you know. In this village one owes absolute obedience to the chief priest. There's something amazingly powerful about the kind of wisdom that arises from people's traditional ways, isn't there? For generations, the priest's wife has been the local midwife. In a village with no doctor, the midwife's knowledge of nursing gives her an enormously important role. So people come to the temple in all matters involving life and death, you see. The mayor is no exception, nor the headmaster, nor the policeman. That's why even a double-dyed villain like me—a Red and a consumptive—can manage to stay alive in these times if he throws himself on the chief priest's mercy. My father has known him since they were at school. Though how someone as wordly as my father maintained his ties with a man like the chief priest is a puzzle to me."

The woman appeared a third time, carrying a large tray. It held dishes of ceremonial red rice, fried eggs, and bracken sprouts boiled in soy.

"Someone's had a baby, have they?" Wakui asked.

"Down at the Nishikuras' son's place. Poor thing'll never know its father, though. They've already been notified that he died in action."

110

Wakui barely went through the motions of eating, then lay back again. "I know I ought to eat, but I can't." Setsuko had taken up her chopsticks at his invitation, but she had no appetite either. Her journey had meant an early start and many changes of train, all of them crowded, and her weariness showed from head to foot, although she was trying to hide it.

"Living here, I've got a lifetime supply of red rice and funeral buns," Wakui laughed.

Perhaps, thought Setsuko, she'd cried that day because his surroundings were *too* normal. Perhaps when the stresses of the abnormal life she'd been enduring day after day met that long-forgotten tranquillity, it had thrown her off balance. It seemed many, many years since she'd lost the peace of mind of a normal way of life. The distance was not only one of time, however; people's hearts had been so hardened and spurred on to hatred of the enemy that there seemed no end to its ravages, nor any way back.

"You're not well yourself, are you?" Wakui spoke from his pillow, with closed eyes. "Your cough has been worrying me ever since you arrived."

"Yes, at the last medical examination I was told I had a shadow on my chest X-ray."

"You were crazy to come all this way."

"But there's something I must give you."

As he accepted the notebooks she held out, Wakui said sadly, "Well, I may not die in an air raid, but I mightn't last much longer, you know. When it comes to who has the right and all that sort of thing, surely I'm no more entitled than you?"

It didn't take long to explain that what she meant by "right" had nothing to do with longevity. As she lay with closed lids in the night that had returned to the shelter, Shōichi Wakui's dark eyes, widening in an intense stare, came back vividly. "And that's why you've come all this way to see me?"

February –

Dear Setsuko,

Papa has died. It happened five days ago. It was his last wish that Mama and I should not be present. Not only that, but he gave strict instructions that his family should not be told until after the cremation. Mama's condition has been poor lately, and since Dr. Ishizuka thought it would be better if I stayed with her, we asked him to go for Papa's ashes. All yesterday and the day before I thought about Papa. You were here when Dr. Ishizuka first brought the news about him, so you know what happened, don't you? The shock of that description made me shake uncontrollably, but I'd been telling myself ever since that it must be lies, absolutely unbelievable lies. But not now. When I heard he'd given instructions that we were not to know anything until he'd been cremated, I believed the doctor's story. In my heart I'm hugging dear Papa, and I don't care if he's blind and toothless and half-bald and thin as a mummy. Poor Papa! How he must have suffered. I love him just as much, no matter how ugly he looked in the end. But I hate the people who made my handsome Papa into such a ghost of himself. I'll curse them as long as I live. When I find out who did it—who changed him like that and then killed him—I'll get revenge on them after I grow up, I swear I will. I'll never give up, no matter how powerful or important they are. I'm burning with anger and hatred. I'm not like Mama, holding Papa's urn and wailing, but deep in my heart I'm vowing vengeance. In the meantime, I'm just bearing it grimly.

Dr. Ishizuka, Mama and I have discussed what to do and decided not to tell anyone of Papa's death or hold a funeral. Although he was a Christian, I don't think there can be any words of God that could comfort his soul.

Setsuko, there's one favor I'd like to ask of you. Next time you come, please let me have a good cry. I want to cry my heart out in your arms. There's so much bottled up that won't come out, it's hurting my chest and I can't breathe.

Five more days. If only you knew how I'm longing for your visit.

Naomi Niwa

"Professor Niwa's case is a little different from mine. He was an economist specializing in the U.S. From our viewpoint he was your typical petit bourgeois. And at first he could simply have retracted what he'd written and escaped the charge of 'thought crimes.' I've got a friend who's in publishing, and for most of the years that I've been rusticating down here he kept me in touch with the outside world, so I know more or less what happened. When relations with America were close to deadlock, Niwa wrote an article saying that war was out of the question, if only because of the superiority of their economic strength. Of course he was writing as an economist, but the editors decided discretion was called for at that point, and they didn't print it. There must have been an informer at work, however, because it came to the army's attention and he was taken into custody. If he'd simply apologized he might have got off, but instead the professor insisted on the correctness of his views. This made matters much, much worse. I heard he'd been placed under long-term detention pending trial. Then my friend received his call-up papers, and I lost track of what happened. So Professor Niwa has died? I can't imagine such a terrible death. Back when we used to visit him at home, he had a very lively little girl—more like a little boy, really. She was always hiding under the professor's desk. A student once dived under there to pick up a pen he'd dropped and they banged heads. What a fuss she made! And you say both his wife and his daughter are dead?"

"Naomi was two years behind me at school, but she taught me a lot of things. I never realized it, though, right to the end. When I started asking myself how Naomi had got into such a pitiful situation, I really couldn't answer. Because I began to see I was in a quite different position, however much I wanted to protect her—in fact it was the existence of people like me that had done that to her. After she died I reread *Les Thibault* and the gray notebook to see if they'd help me find the answer. I think that all I did was make Naomi unhappy."

"No, I think you're wrong there. Just glancing through the notebook, it's obvious that Naomi trusted you deeply. And that you completely lived up to her trust. In the old days I used to be skeptical about there being a genuine unity that rose above people's circumstances. But, living here for so long, I've learned that the masses can't be contained in books—they're too great. We're all in this together, whatever we think of one another. In the last analysis we all have our humanity in common."

"But I'm a hypocrite. In my heart I thought Naomi's father was a traitor, just like the Akiyamas did, and yet I kept trying to defend her. I never had any right to her friendship in the first place."

"Don't be so quick to blame yourself. At your age it's not surprising that you thought Professor Niwa a traitor. What *is* surprising is that a girl like you exists at all in this day and age. I could understand it in someone like Naomi, who grew up in an unusual environment, but according to what she's written here you were even an exemplary student at school, weren't you?"

"I was always trying to be a good girl. In front of Naomi, too. And at this moment I'm trying to seem like a good girl for you. I've no right to be talking with you like this, and yet I try to make out that I'm one of you."

"That's no way to talk. Now listen to me: I've been thinking lately that to the people, individually, war is like a storm. It arrives unwanted, smashes their lives, and then suddenly blows over. We, the people, are the ones who sustain and carry on the war, but we're not the ones who begin or end it. You and I are in the same position—two individuals trapped by the system. The only difference is that I've lived longer and had time to work out my own ideas till I know what I want, and you haven't. But you've been thinking and asking questions for yourself while you experience war—not the way I did, as knowledge in books, but as a reality. And as long as you have that questioning attitude, I think you've been the best friend Naomi could have had."

"That makes me feel much better. But it doesn't matter any more, anyway—it's all over. Naomi is dead, and I've delivered her mother's notebooks to you, which is a load off my mind. And I've made my decision."

"What decision is that?"

"I've decided to fight to the last as a Japanese, and to share the fate of the nation."

"That's crazy. How can you, when you understand so clearly what's happening? As I see it, the war's about to end. It won't be long now. You probably believe this is a war for justice, but there's no such thing as a war fought purely over ideals. Because in the end it's a power struggle. A power struggle for economic control. They'll shout their slogans about its sacredness and a hundred million glorious deaths, just as long as it's the common people whose lives are at stake, but when it's their turn, and the imperial system and the state itself—the justification for all their actions—come under threat, then there's no reason for them to continue the war. Ōizumi-san, it won't be long now. The war will end. So wait, be patient till then. When the war is over, there'll be work crying out for fine young people like you."

"You're entitled to think about what comes after the war. I'm not. Since I was a child I've been writing letters to soldiers at the front saying 'Please fight with all your might. I'll defend the home front

115

with my life.' And I'm still making vacuum tubes every day for Japan, for victory. I don't know exactly how my vacuum tubes are helping win the war, but all the same, I have no right to run away at this stage. I have no choice but to go on believing what I've believed till now."

"I know too well who made you believe it. And the fault lies not with you for believing, but with those who persuaded you. But the men who indoctrinated you are certainly not going to take responsibility for what they've done. They'll calmly betray you when the time comes."

"No, they won't. Our leaders would never betray the people. I'll never believe that."

February –

Dear Naomi,

It seems my letter hasn't reached you. The mail is affected by air raids, too, I suppose. Well, it can't be helped. As you may have guessed, my cold is still hanging on. I can make it to work, but on Saturday night I always come down with a fever and have to spend Sunday in bed. I was coughing so badly I couldn't have gone out, even though I knew you had to nurse your mother and so we wouldn't be able to meet otherwise. I'm sorry. I promise I'll come next Sunday.

I've read over what you wrote last time, again and again. But I don't know what I can say in return. Any condolences I might offer seem empty. It was a great shock to me, too, though not to be compared with what it must have meant to you. I've reread the volumes of Les Thibault *you lent me last time, especially the part that takes place in the summer of 1914. I've been thinking about what it means to risk your life to oppose war, like Jacques*

Thibault and your father. I'm fighting at the risk of my life to bring this sacred war to completion. What's the sense of the two of us giving our lives to opposite causes? I don't know. I just feel as though I'm out of my depth and floundering in some enormous shock. Perhaps as an older friend I should advise you against swearing vengeance for your father, as you're still just a little girl. But I couldn't do that. I understand the violence of your anger, and I have a feeling you may be right. Look at me sitting on the fence: my own position leaves me speechless.

I can't take your hand and share your anger, Naomi, nor swear vengeance with you. Here am I, driving myself—in spite of my cold—to boost production for the sacred war effort. So while I claim to understand your anger and grief, I'm actually pulling with all my might in the opposite direction, day after day, in the belief that what I'm doing is right.

To tell the truth, I don't understand a thing. I can't help feeling that I had no right to call myself your friend, though I made out I was, and pretended my friendship was the best thing for you.

Please forgive me, Naomi. Perhaps being sick is just an excuse because I haven't the courage to see you.

Setsuko Ōizumi

Before she knew what was happening, she could hardly breathe. She forgot all else as she tore her jacket open and loosened her waist string, seeking some relief from the restriction. The air in the shelter was certainly stale, but she was suffocating as if there were no air left.

"Wait here with me till the war is over. If you stay here, you'll be better by then." The sound of Shōichi Wakui's voice brought a great rush of air, and with it the rustle of a breeze in the bamboo grove

117

behind the temple building. "Kiyo! This young lady's another invalid. Would you take her on too?"

"If the chief priest says so, I'll have to, won't I? A consumptive taking a consumptive bride and sleeping in the temple—what a match!" Setsuko, already on her feet in readiness to leave, had stopped short at the woman's loud and pitiless laugh. Though she knew it was impossible to stay, she couldn't deny a reluctance to leave this scene of everyday normality.

Shōichi Wakui was as startled as Setsuko by the woman's jibe. "What nonsense! Don't mind her, she's a bit touched." The moment brought Setsuko sharply to her senses, reminding her of the distance between Wakui and herself. She would never have dreamed of visiting him if it hadn't been for Naomi. And even to Naomi she'd been a distant figure at best, a realization that hurt Setsuko very much. She was grateful to Wakui, for in the few short hours they'd known each other he had been quick to see the pain in her heart and quick to offer consolation.

Comforted, Setsuko fell into a light sleep. Her breathing was no easier. An invisible dark vapor was quietly gathering around her, the darkness thickening as each new layer settled though the gas itself was transparent. Sinking inert to the bottom, Setsuko breathed in tiny gasps.

"Can't I change your mind?" The sun was in the west, and the broad corridor along the south side of the temple hall held a moment's peace before twilight. Wakui was leaning against a pillar of the high roof, the big feather pillow at his back and his eyes closed. His long outstretched feet were dazzlingly white. When was it that Hajime's feet had dazzled her like that?

"You've no reason to rush to your death."

"I have no right to live on after the war ends."

"Isn't it more valuable to know that, and live through what's about

118

to happen in that knowledge? Only people like you will truly be able to tell what to do after the war."

There was a large loquat tree in the courtyard, its tiny fruit massed beneath thick foliage on many branches. A partridge flew up from the treetop with a bright cry.

"What a pity—if you'd come a month later, you could have had some loquats." Shōichi Wakui raised his eyes and gazed after the bird. "Until a year or so ago I used to climb this tree when Kiyo wasn't looking and pick loquats warmed by the sun, as many as I could reach, starting with the plumpest ones. I knew I could have had them served for dessert, washed and chilled in water from the well, but climbing the tree and picking them myself was the best part." When, after a short silence, he added "I can't do that now," there was a note of despair in his voice.

Trapped under endlessly falling layers of clear darkness, Setsuko saw her body grow rigid. She could not move her head or her limbs; only her lungs continued their last faint gasps. Here and there in their smooth red contours she could see round shadows where the invading bacilli had created cavities. With each painful heave, blood oozed into the holes and collected, then flowed through narrow channels to the bronchi. The bronchi convulsed, attempting to expel the puddles, but more gathered. Setsuko had her eyes closed, yet they needed closing over again, for the sight of her lungs and bronchi heaving inside her chest was too cruel. But however tightly she closed them, the image returned behind the lids.

"I don't think there's another creature on earth as tough as a human being. A people never dies out with its country. When all else is lost, as long as there are people left alive, the future can be placed in their hands. Value your life, Ōizumi-san." When the car came to take her to the station, Shōichi Wakui walked her to the temple gate, leaning on a stick. "It's against my principles, you know—to shorten my life by coming to see you off!" He chuckled at his own expense, then went on imploringly: "You must understand why I've come outside even though it's bad for me." He folded his hands over the knob of his cane, rested his chin heavily on them, and breathed hard. "Please believe me. There will be a time after the war when you can really live. Believe in that and value your life." The dark invisible layers were piling up. They filled the confined space of the shelter, covered it, and enveloped earth and sky. Setsuko's sleep grew gradually deeper, her breathing shallower and gentler.

April –

Dear Setsuko,

April is here. You didn't come once during March. I know you're not well, but you're not taking time off from the factory, and I did so wish you'd spare me just one day. You've probably noticed that I've torn out a lot of pages before starting this one. Can you guess what was on them? Yes, bitter reproaches because you're so cold to me. But today I tore them all out and burned them in the yard. Tomorrow I'm going to visit you. I've asked Dr. Ishizuka for a nurse to take over for the day. Tomorrow I'll give you this notebook as I leave and ask you to read it when I've gone. You must know by now—I've made up my mind to come tomorrow and say goodbye.

I thought I'd have you to turn to after Papa died. I thought you'd be as angry and sad as I was. But it didn't work out that way.

Now I understand what a nuisance I've been. I think I wanted you to accept me no matter what I did. But, Setsuko, please believe this: I still love you. And that's why I mustn't presume so much on your kindness. You've been my friend for a year now. You've been very important to me all that time, and you always will be.

But that doesn't matter. I've decided to say goodbye. Because

I've understood that if I go on taking advantage of your kindness I'll only make you unhappy.

I've also given up the idea of revenge for Papa. I could never have carried it out anyway, because I won't live long enough to be an adult. But that doesn't matter either. The sooner I die the sooner I can see Papa. I wonder what he looks like in heaven? Of course, I don't mind if he still looks awful, but I'd rather see my old handsome Papa again.

Setsuko, I wish with all my heart I'd been born in an age without war. Why do people go to war, when we're all the same human beings? I've been looking at a globe, and thinking as I spin it round. There were no dividing lines on the Earth's surface when it was formed. Who thought them up? How happy we could be if we erased the lines and were simply people, not Japanese or Americans or Chinese. If we could live anywhere, with anyone, in peace.

Thank you very much for all your kindness to me. Please keep Les Thibault *as a small reminder of our friendship. Do your best for the country and don't worry about me.*

Naomi Niwa

Setsuko was wandering in that dark, clear space. The far distance was in total darkness, but a glimmer of light appeared closer at hand as she moved forward, forward, in search of something. It could have been a sound, perhaps a spoken word. She couldn't tell where it came from. She had no idea how far the dark invisible layers extended, or what lay ahead. The unknown sound had come from somewhere to stir the depths of her soul and rekindle a flicker of life. As Setsuko gradually regained consciousness, the sound of whistling came clearly to her ears. "Hajime!" The whistle came from outside the shelter—there was no mistaking it. A last reserve of strength roused her from deepest sleep. "Hajime!" She called on all her remaining energy to crawl toward the shelter door. She hauled herself up the steps, by her arms alone. "Hajime!" A figure was standing in the open daylight. It was indistinct, but it was definitely where the whistling came from. "Hajime!" Her voice was barely audible. The figure seemed to sense her presence, though, for the whistling stopped. The figure said something. Something. Not in Japanese. The figure standing beside the shelter in the ruins by the Katabira River, whistling a Scottish air to the sky, was an American soldier —one of the very first to land in Japan. Setsuko slid down onto the shelter floor. She would never move again.

定価3,000円

in Japan